Praise for
What's Stopping You?

"Bruce Barringer and Duane Ireland's new book, *What's Stopping You?* is an insightful and thought-provoking examination of nine common myths that discourage individuals from starting new businesses. ... This book is much-needed and long overdue.... The value of *What's Stopping You?* is that it effectively debunks the false premises that too often preclude acts of business start up. *What's Stopping You?* is an encouraging, instructive, and eloquently written book that would be a valuable addition to any aspiring entrepreneur's bookshelf."

Jeffrey G. Covin, Samuel and Pauline Glaubinger Professor of Entrepreneurship, Kelley School of Business, Indiana University, Bloomington, Indiana

"Over the years I have observed many seemingly great business opportunities never get off the ground. Quite often, what holds these aspiring entrepreneurs back are common misconceptions about the difficulties and risks of starting a new business. In *What's Stopping You?*, Professors Barringer and Ireland systematically break down the myths that hold many entrepreneurs back from pursuing their dreams."

Jeffrey R. Cornwall, The Jack C. Massey Chair in Entrepreneurship, Belmont University, Nashville, Tennessee

"Barringer and Ireland simultaneously demystify start-up misconceptions and empower readers to explore their own opportunity with renewed passion. Many prospective entrepreneurs feel trapped by myths, the authors carefully detail the myth's fallacies and encourage the reader to see beyond start-up stereotypes. Future and experienced entrepreneurs have much to learn from *What's Stopping You?*"

Sarah Schupp, Founder/CEO, University Parent Media, Boulder, Colorado

"Creating your own business from scratch can be a mental, emotional, and financial roller coaster ride. Bruce Barringer and Duane Ireland's book provides a 'voice of reason' and helps give you the confidence to realize you can do it. They recognize that starting a business is hard work, but that it is attainable—and that you should celebrate your accomplishments every step of the way."

Jan Stephenson Kelly, Cofounder/CEO, Spark Craft Studios, Cambridge, MA

WHAT'S STOPPING YOU?

Shatter the 9 Most Common Myths Keeping You from Starting Your Own Business

Bruce R. Barringer, PhD
R. Duane Ireland, PhD

Vice President, Publisher: Tim Moore
Associate Publisher and Director of Marketing: Amy Neidlinger
Acquisitions Editor: Jennifer Simon
Editorial Assistant: Pamela Boland
Development Editor: Russ Hall
Operations Manager: Gina Kanouse
Digital Marketing Manager: Julie Phifer
Assistant Marketing Manager: Megan Colvin
Cover Designer: Chuti Prasertsith
Managing Editor: Kristy Hart
Copy Editor: Language Logistics
Proofreader: Anne Goebel
Indexer: Erika Millen
Senior Compositor: Gloria Schurick
Manufacturing Buyer: Dan Uhrig

FT Press offers excellent discounts on this book when ordered in quantity for bulk purchases or special sales. For more information, please contact U.S. Corporate and Government Sales, 1-800-382-3419, corpsales@pearsontechgroup.com. For sales outside the U.S., please contact International Sales at international@pearson.com.

Company and product names mentioned herein are the trademarks or registered trademarks of their respective owners.

Printed in the United States of America

First Printing May 2008

ISBN-10: 0-13-244457-7
ISBN-13: 978-0-13-244457-6

Pearson Education LTD.
Pearson Education Australia PTY, Limited.
Pearson Education Singapore, Pte. Ltd.
Pearson Education North Asia, Ltd.
Pearson Education Canada, Ltd.
Pearson Educatión de Mexico, S.A. de C.V.
Pearson Education—Japan
Pearson Education Malaysia, Pte. Ltd.

Library of Congress Cataloging-in-Publication Data

Barringer, Bruce R.

What's stopping you? : shatter the 9 most common myths keeping you from starting your own business / Bruce Barringer, Duane Ireland.

p. cm.

ISBN 0-13-244457-7 (pbk. : alk. paper) 1. New business enterprises. 2. Entrepreneurship. 3. Self-employed. 4. Small business. I. Ireland, Duane. II. Title.

HD62.5.B366 2008

658.1'1—dc22

2007049589

To Janet, John, Jennifer, and Emily:
The love and support of a family is a wonderful thing.
—Bruce Barringer

To Mary Ann: Thank you for your never-ending support,
love, and nurturing for all of these years. I love you.
—R. Duane Ireland

C O N T E N T S

Preface . . . . *ix*

PART I: GETTING STARTED—
IT MAY NOT BE AS HARD AS YOU THINK   1

Chapter 1: *Myth No. 1: It Takes an Extraordinary Person to Start a Business;*
Truth No. 1: You Can Do It! 3

Chapter 2: *Myth No. 2: Starting a Business Involves Lots of Risk;*
Truth No. 2: It May Not Be as Risky as You Think 23

Chapter 3: *Myth No. 3: It Takes a Lot of Money to Start a Business;*
Truth No. 3: It Might Not Cost as Much as You Think 43

Chapter 4: *Myth No. 4: It Takes a Great Deal of Business Experience to Start a Successful Businesses;*
Truth No. 4: Successful Businesses Are Started by People with All Levels of Business Experience 67

Chapter 5: *Myth No. 5: The Best Business Ideas Are Already Taken;*
Truth No. 5: There Are an Infinite Number of Possibilities for Good Business Ideas 87

PART II: RUNNING AND GROWING A BUSINESS—
DON'T UNDERESTIMATE YOUR CHANCES   111

Chapter 6: *Myth No. 6: No One Can Compete Against Wal-Mart and the Other Big-Box Retailers;*
Truth No. 6: You Can Compete Against the Big-Box Retailers if You Have the Right Plan 113

Chapter 7: *Myth No. 7: It's Almost Impossible for a New Business to Get Noticed;*
Truth No. 7: There Are Many Ways for New Businesses to Get Noticed and Recognized 133

Chapter 8: *Myth No. 8: The Internet Isn't What It Was All Hyped Up to Be;*
Truth No. 8: There Are Many Legitimate and Enjoyable Ways to Make Money Online 157

Chapter 9: *Myth No. 9: It's Easy to Start a Business, But It's Difficult and Stressful to Grow One;*
Truth No. 9: Businesses Can Be Grown Profitably and Enjoyably 179

Index 205

ABOUT THE AUTHORS

Bruce R. Barringer, PhD is an Associate Professor at the University of Central Florida. The author of two small business/entrepreneurship textbooks, Barringer's work is read worldwide. He is also the author of the *Wall Street Journal's Entrepreneurship Weekly Review*, which is distributed to small business and entrepreneurship teachers and students across the United States.

R. Duane Ireland, PhD is Professor of Management and holds the Foreman R. and Ruby S. Bennett Chair in Business in the Mays Business School at Texas A&M University. He is the author of entrepreneurship and strategic management textbooks that are widely sold throughout the world. He teaches entrepreneurship to executive MBA students and has consulted with a variety of small and large organizations.

PREFACE

Have you ever caught yourself daydreaming while at work and wondering if what you're doing is all you'll achieve in your career? Or has your heart ever ached to meet a certain desire, like completing work that you truly enjoy, being your own boss, making more money, or being home when your kids get out of school?

These types of thoughts and desires confront people every day—even those with seemingly perfect jobs. In response, most people just sigh or shrug and accept life as it is. But not always. A growing number of people from all walks of life are starting their own businesses as a way of improving their lives. In fact, there are roughly 15 million self-employed people in the United States today. But there is a problem. The problem is that because some business owners have hit it rich and made a large impact on society, there is a growing tendency to view business owners as bigger-than-life and place them in the same category as professional athletics and rock stars. This tendency has led to the prevailing wisdom that starting a business is an extremely difficult task and that a person must have "loads of money" and "tons of talent" to get a new business off the ground.

While it's true that some businesses are difficult to start and that talent and money are needed to get a business off the ground, many of the tales and perceptions about the enormous difficulties associated with starting a business are just myths. The truth is that the ability to start a successful business is much more within the average person's reach than the myths allow us to believe. If you have the interest it took to pick up this book, chances are you have the talent, the money, and the character needed to start and run a business of your own.

Who Is This Book Written For?

This book is for anyone who has thought about starting his own business but has been reluctant to try. This group covers a wide spectrum, from people who have an idea for a new business but are uneasy about leaving their current jobs to people who are dissatisfied with their jobs or careers but feel trapped. It also includes people who have a goal or want to live a particular lifestyle and see starting a business as the most reasonable way to make it happen.

Although some people do start businesses, most of the people in these categories think about it occasionally but set their thoughts aside because of the anxiety and worry caused by the nine myths that we discuss in the book. It's hard to blame them. Listen to the first three myths and ask yourself if they would discourage you from starting a business: Myth 1: It takes an extraordinary person to start a business; Myth 2: Starting a business involves lots of risk; Myth 3: It takes a lot of money to start a business. Pretty daunting list, isn't it? And there are six myths to go!

A potentially rewarding part of reading this book are the many people you meet that objectively aren't any smarter, richer, or more gifted than you. What they do have that you probably don't is a successful business startup. As we progress together through the chapters of the book, we knock off the myths one by one by showing how ordinary people prove that they simply aren't true. But there are exceptions. In most cases, it does take an extraordinary person and lots of money to launch a biotechnology, a medical products, or a semiconductor firm. But these cases, by far, are the exception rather than the rule. You'll be amazed what people are able to accomplish with very little money and the simple common sense that is the foundation on which many of the business startups described in this book were built.

What Will You Learn by Reading This Book?

Next time you go to a bookstore or are in an airport gift shop, try this little experiment: Spend a few minutes watching people browse through the business magazines or books. Watch their faces and try to guess what their circumstances are. If you're like us, in the majority of instances, you'll get the feeling that they're looking for answers. There is some problem or unmet need in their personal or professional lives that they'd like to resolve but can't figure out how to on their own. So they're scanning the books for potential answers. If you conduct this experiment long enough, we can almost guarantee you that you'll see the ultimate example of this scenario play out. Someone will be scanning the shelves of business books and will come across a book that immediately catches her attention. The person will then intently page through the book for a few minutes, in a state of total concentration, and a slight sign of hope or relief will gradually start to cross his or her face. As the person proceeds to the checkout counter, he or she will be clutching the book as if it were a $1,000 bill. You can't help but hope, for that person's sake, that his or her question has just been answered.

This experiment is a reminder of how desperate people are for answers to the problems or challenges in their lives and how much hope, information, and potential help books can offer. If you're reading this preface, you're probably tired of your job, want to make more money, desire to pursue the career you have always wanted, or are thinking about starting your own business for a reason equally important to you. What's stopping you, if you're similar to most of the people we talk to, is a lack of knowledge about the business startup process and nervousness about one or more of the topics covered by our nine myths. This set of circumstances leads to a lack of self-confidence, which researchers believe is the number one reason that people hesitate to start their own firms.

What you will learn by reading this book is the truth about many of the most important aspects of starting a business. Our goals are to educate you and stir your emotions. We hope that as you read the book, you'll pause from time to time and think to yourself, "That's interesting—perhaps I have been too quick to dismiss the idea of starting my own business." We also pledge that the stories will be compelling enough that you'll stop occasionally to excitedly tell a coworker or friend things like, "Do you know it's not true that nine out of ten new businesses fail?" (In truth, 66% of new businesses are still operating after two years, and 50% survive four years or more.) Or you'll want to share stories such as, "You won't believe how this woman I just read about quit her job as a general partner in an investment firm to buy an adventure travel company. She didn't do it because she could make more money—she did it to lead a more satisfying and enjoyable life."

How Is This Book Organized?

The book is organized into nine chapters—one chapter for each of the nine myths. Each chapter starts by stating the myth and the corresponding truth and is followed by a complete discussion of the chapter's topic. Each chapter contains two to three special features that add to the material in the chapter. Although the book is admittedly upbeat, we paint a realistic job preview for those who are thinking about becoming a business owner. We want people to be realistic about their prospects, but we also want them to be confident and to think, "I can do this. It's not beyond my reach."

We now invite you to enjoy learning about the myths associated with starting your own business and to learn from the lessons in this book. If you are inspired by a particular story in the book, if you would like to tell us your start-up story, or if you are impacted by this book in any way, please feel free to e-mail us your story at story@mythsbook.com. We would love to hear from you. Much of what we know we learn from people just like you. We'd love to consider including your story in future books as we work together to dispel the myths and reveal the truth about the business start-up process.

PART I

*Getting Started—It May Not Be as
Hard as You Think*

Myth No. 1:
It Takes an Extraordinary Person to Start a Business

Truth No. 1:
You Can Do It!

Introduction

The notion that it takes an extraordinary person to start a business is the most damaging myth that we discuss in this book. In most cases, it simply isn't true. There are two ways to think about this myth. First, ordinary people, no richer or smarter than you, start new businesses every day. To convince you of this, we'll introduce you to some of these people in this chapter and throughout the book. Second, even if the myth were true, who's to say that you're not extraordinary? No one has the exact same set of abilities, skills, values, experiences, past accomplishments, and personal aspirations that you do. As a result, you could be more uniquely qualified or have a more compelling reason to start a specific business than someone with a PhD from an Ivy League school or 20 years of executive work experience.

If you accept that these sentiments are true, it can totally transform your attitude about whether you're capable of starting a business. It can free you to start thinking about whether specific business opportunities are right for you rather than whether you're capable of starting a business at all. It can also boost your morale and sense of self-esteem. Starting a business isn't easy, but neither are many things in life that are worth pursuing. The brutal reality of life is that in most instances what we're able to accomplish boils down to whether we believe we can do it or not, the amount of encouragement and support we get, and the degree to which we're willing to work hard and get help. As you'll see throughout this chapter, there is no aspect of life in which this set of realities is truer than in the case of starting your own business.

The differences between people who start their own businesses from those who don't has been studied for years. The somewhat surprising collection of results illustrate that there are no meaningful differences between business owners and nonbusiness owners in the most basic human characteristics, behaviors, attitudes, and desires.[1] Most people, for example, want to make more money and crave independence, not just people who start their own businesses. Similarly, in regard to personality traits, people who start their own businesses are just as diverse as people who work in traditional jobs. You don't have to have a certain personality, behave in a particular way, or have a certain set of motives or desires to be a successful business owner.

What type of person, then, do you have to be to start and run your own successful business? Say you're a 50-year-old male whose career has plateaued, and you see no chance for advancement, or you're a 28-year-old female with two small children, and it literally breaks your heart to drop them off at daycare five mornings a week. What type of people are able to say, "Stop, I'm not doing this anymore. There is another option—I'm starting my own business to take control of my life, set my priorities straight, and do something that makes sense for me and that I'll be able to thoroughly enjoy."

The myth that "it takes an extraordinary person to start a business" is damaging in part because it focuses strictly on the individual. If you believe it, it puts the entire burden on you, rather than the broader set of circumstances and issues involved. It causes you to think, either consciously or subconsciously, "Am I good enough?" or "Do I have what it takes?"

Thinking this way invariably leads to an up or down vote in your mind—you decide, once and for all, whether you're good enough or not good enough to start a business based on your notion of what an "extraordinary person" is. This type of thinking is fundamentally flawed. Objectively, most of us don't know if we have the skills, abilities, aptitude, and experience necessary to tackle a specific task or do a particular job unless we learn more about it (or have done it or something similar to it before). In addition, nearly all of us would seek the advice of others and ask their opinions about our suitability for a particular business or career before making the final decision to start our own businesses. In some cases, we may even decide to go back to school or get additional training if we're interested in a particular area but don't think our skills are sufficient. So in reality, the issue of whether you're good enough to start a business doesn't depend just on *you* at a fixed point in time. It depends on a lot of things. Primarily, it depends on the *fit* between your skills, abilities, experiences, and aspirations and the demands of the particular business you have in mind. It also depends on whether you really *want* to start a business or not.

There are basically four types of businesses, as shown in Table 1.1.

Table 1.1   Types of Businesses

Type of Business	Explanation	Examples
Survival	A business that provides its owner just enough money to put food on the table	Handyman, lawn service, part-time childcare and pay bills
Lifestyle	A business that provides its owner the opportunity to pursue a certain lifestyle and make a living at it	Home-based eBay business, sub-shop, single-unit franchise, clothing boutique, personal trainer
Managed Growth	A business that employs 10 or more people, may have several outlets, and may be introducing new products or services to the market	Multi-unit franchise, regional restaurant chain, Web retailer (modest scale)
Aggressive Growth	A business that is bringing new products and services to the market and has aggressive growth plans	Computer software, medical equipment, Web retailer (large scale), national restaurant chain

All these types of businesses are acceptable—there is no value judgment made here. This book, however, focuses on the last three: lifestyle, managed growth, and aggressive growth firms. A natural outcome of the myth that it takes an extraordinary person to start a business is the mistaken belief that every business should grow rapidly and make a lot of money. There are many small businesses that provide their owners financial security and satisfying lives and never grow or make tons of money. This book equally targets this type of business along with more aggressive growth firms.

In our experience, at least four primary factors prompt and motivate people to start their own business. As you read through these factors, tip your chair back from time to time and think about your own life and the degree to which each of these factors might play a role in your own decision to start a business. Pay particular attention to the examples of people who left traditional jobs to start their own businesses and the reasons they made the decisions they did.

Factors That Prompt and Motivate a Person to Start His or Her Own Business

The factors that prompt and motivate people to start their own businesses are shown in Figure 1.1. A person's decision to start a business is both practical and personal. It's practical in that the decision is based partly on a simple calculation of whether a person can better manage her life and meet her aspirations and goals through a traditional job or by owning a business. It's personal in that the decision also hinges on whether a person believes she is capable of owning a business or not, whether she has the support of the most important people in her life, and the degree of passion she has for a particular business idea.

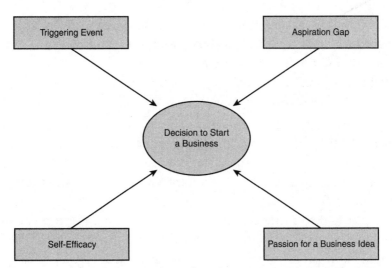

Figure 1.1   *Factors That Prompt and Motivate a Person to Start His or Her Own Business*

Let's look at the four factors that prompt and motivate someone to start a business.

Triggering Event

There is almost always a triggering event that starts someone thinking about starting a business. A triggering event can be getting a business idea, either by deliberate search or chance encounter, or it can be any incident or occurrence that has an impact on a person and causes him to think about making a major life change—like changing a job or career. Examples of triggering events, which can be either positive or negative, are shown in Table 1.2.

Table 1.2   Triggering Events

Positive	Negative
New business idea	Job loss
Birth of first child	Passed up for a promotion at work
All children are now in school	Need to transfer to a less desirable location
Last child has left home (empty nest)	Undesirable changes at work
Inheritance	Serious health issue
Personal milestone (40th birthday)	Death in family
Retirement	Major national trauma (9/11)

For many people, the types of events shown in Table 1.2 have little impact, at least as far as their jobs or careers are concerned, and don't trigger any reaction. For others, one or more of these events might be deeply impacting and cause them to seriously consider making changes in their lifestyles and careers.

An example of how an event can trigger a major change in a person's life, which leads to the decision to start a business, is provided by Sean Tennant, a middle-aged male. After a 20-year career with Delta Airlines, Tennant had to decide whether to take a pay cut to stay in Boston or transfer to Atlanta, a Delta hub. "I had to make a decision whether to go and get a cheap buyout (equivalent to three months' salary) or stay with a sinking Titanic and get nothing," Tennant recalls.[2] He decided to leave Delta and buy a Cartridge World franchise. Cartridge World is a rapidly growing franchise organization that refills ink cartridges for about half the price a new cartridge costs. An added benefit of owning a Cartridge World franchise, from Tennant's perspective, is that it encourages people to recycle ink cartridges rather than replace them, a practice that appeals to his sense of environmental stewardship. Tennant now owns and runs a busy Cartridge World franchise and indicated that his business started breaking after only four months.

Sometimes a Trigger Event Must Wait Until the "Timing Is Right" for a New Business to Be Launched

Although the term "triggering event" implies that an event immediately triggers a person's interest in starting a business, that doesn't mean the business starts right away. Sometimes people mull over the impact of an event for some time, or there are other reasons why the business might not start immediately. This happened to Dave Long, one of the cofounders of Screen Life, the company that makes the popular DVD board game, Scene It?, a game in which players answer trivia questions about films or pop culture.

In 1992, Long and his wife, Kelly, hosted a Halloween party in their San Diego home. To do something different, Long came up with the idea of putting together a videotape that featured scenes from various Halloween-themed moves. Short scenes played until someone shouted out the title of the film. The game was a hit. The next day Long and his wife got together with two of their guests from the night before to talk about converting the idea into a commercial product. Unfortunately, they quickly discovered an insurmountable obstacle—the linear nature of the VHS format. It's not possible on a video tape to quickly jump from scene to scene or to stop a scene (when someone gets the right answer) and quickly move to the next scene. They decided to shelve the idea until technology provided a better solution.

In October 2000, Long bought a DVD player, and all of a sudden his idea of eight years prior didn't seem so far-fetched anymore. The DVD format allows for much more flexibility than video tapes by allowing users to jump from scene to scene quickly and conveniently. Long partnered with Craig Kinzer, a game enthusiast, and after some experimentation and lots of help from others, Scene It? was born. They formed their new company and introduced the game to the marketplace in 2002, 10 years after the Halloween party where the whole idea began.[3]

Aspiration Gap

The second factor that prompts people to begin thinking about starting a business is the presence of one or more aspiration gaps in their lives. All of us have aspirations, which are made up of our most important goals, objectives, ambitions, desires, and longings. Our aspirations vary because they are influenced by our values, abilities, experiences, families, jobs, and individual circumstances. When one or more of our aspirations are unmet, we have *aspiration gaps* in our lives. The extent to which an aspiration gap prompts someone to take action, to try to eliminate or narrow the gap, varies based on the importance of the aspiration and the individual involved.

Collectively, our aspirations form what researchers call our *aspiration vector*, which is the sum total of all of our aspirations. Sometimes, our aspiration vectors can get complex, particularly during busy times in our lives, like when we're simultaneously trying to build a career, love our spouse, raise kids, save money, stay fit, and so forth. For people who have strong aspirations and are insistent that certain aspirations are met, their aspirations become the motivating or driving factors in their lives. For example, a young mother might have the following three aspirations regarding a job that are particularly important to her: pays at least $40,000 per year, has her home by 3:00 pm on weekdays to meet the school bus, and allows her Sundays to be free to participate in church and volunteer-related activities. Similarly, an Assistant Manager for a large retail chain, like Target or Lowe's, might be driven primarily by the single aspiration of having his own store to manage and run by the time he is 35.

A person can become discouraged or upset when he or she looks at his or her job or alternative jobs in the traditional labor market and concludes that none of the choices will allow his or her most important aspirations to be met. In these instances, a logical alternative is to start a business. Although starting a business isn't easier than a traditional job, a business owner often has more discretion and control over his or her time and schedule. This rationale explains in part the recent jump in the number of home-based businesses. Home-based businesses often help people better juggle both professional and family-related goals and aspirations.

Daryn Kagan, a former reporter for CNN, become discouraged with her career trajectory and decided to leave the cable network to do something she had thought about for a long time, create a Web cast (a streaming video on a Web site) that features good news.

"After 12 years at CNN, it became clear that I wasn't going to have the kind of opportunities that I wanted. I see that as the nudge I needed to move on. I had been thinking of some version of this (business) for a long time. These are the kind of stories I have been drawn to—the kind that make your heart go zing. It was one of those moments in your life where you have a chance to sit back and think, 'If I could do anything in my life, what would it be?'"[4]

After leaving CNN, Kagan eliminated her aspiration gap and fulfilled her ambition by launching darynkagan.com. If you'd like to see the fruits of her efforts, you can go to her Web site and view her daily "good news" Web cast. The stories she posts are both heartfelt and inspiring.

An example of three people who shared an aspiration gap and eliminated it by starting a business together is the story of Christopher Jones, David LaBat, and Mary McGrath. The three, who are educational psychologists, had secure jobs at a public school in the Santa Clarita Valley, north of Los Angeles. Over time, they felt inhibited by the limited range of services they were able to provide students in a school setting; so they left their jobs to start Dynamic Interventions, a more full-service educational psychology and counseling center:

> *"The idea came from some general frustrations with not being able to practice the breadth of service that [we wanted to]," Jones said. "And instead of going to work and being angry about it for the next 30 years, we decided to do something about it. With Dynamic Interventions, our service doesn't stop at the end of the school day. We can go more in-depth and be more beneficial to the whole family."[5]*

Dynamic Interventions now offers a full range of educational and counseling services for school-aged children and their families.

A final example is Kristina O'Connell, who experienced a triggering event and an aspiration gap at the same time, which led her to start Wadee, an online company that sells handmade children's toys and gift items. A former high-tech marketing executive, O'Connell comments on the set of circumstances that motivated her to start her own business:

> *"In 2000, I lost both my parents. That, on top of the fact that I started having children, changed my perspective. It made me realize how short life is, so you've got to do what you love. I had run out of gas with high-tech and was burnt out, so at the end of 2002, I decided to take a couple of years off and start Wadee. I wanted to be home with my family, so I built my business around my family. My husband has been tremendously supportive, and that has allowed me the freedom to follow my passion."[6]*

Even though she was a successful high-tech executive, O'Connell had a long-time interest in starting a company to make children's toys. That interest, or aspiration, coupled with the loss of her parents and the start of her own family, provided her the necessary motivation to set her high-tech career aside and fulfill her aspiration to launch her business.

Self-Efficacy

A third factor that prompts people to start their own businesses is *self-efficacy.* Self-efficacy is similar to self-confidence and refers to the strength of a person's belief that he or she is capable of successfully completing a task.[7] A person generally avoids tasks where his sense of self-efficacy is low and engages in tasks where self-efficacy is high. It's important to understand the distinction between self-efficacy and self-esteem. Self-esteem refers to a person's overall sense of self-worth, whereas self-efficacy refers to a person's ability to complete a specific task. As a result, a person could have a very poor self-efficacy for performing a specific task, like playing golf, but still have a very high self-esteem, if playing golf isn't an activity that's very important to the person's overall sense of self-worth.

The result of this rationale is that a perfectly normal person with a healthy sense of self-esteem could have very low self-efficacy for starting a business. Low self-efficacy often leads people to believe that a task is harder than it is. It also affects how a person deals with a task. Individuals with high self-efficacy for a given task, like starting a business, usually approach it with enthusiasm and drive, while people with a low self-efficacy for the same task approach it with skepticism and dread.[8] This is why some people, even though they often think about starting their own businesses, have never done it. Deep down inside, they believe that they don't have the skills and abilities to start and run a successful business.

Four factors that affect a person's self-efficacy for starting a business (or performing any task) are explained in Table 1.3: experience, modeling, social persuasions, and physiological factors. A person can increase his or her self-efficacy for starting a business by strengthening themselves in one or more of these areas. Simply reading the stories of ordinary people who start and run successful businesses is one form of modeling (or vicarious learning) and can provide you with the sense that "If they can do it, I can do it, too!" Similarly, participating in small business workshops and events where you get encouragement from successful business owners, who are no smarter or more capable than you, can boost your self-efficacy for starting a business of your own.

Table 1.3   Factors Affecting Your Self-Efficacy in Starting a Business

Factor	Explanation
Experience	Experience starting a business or working in a field closely related to the business that you are interested in starting boosts your self-efficacy.
Modeling	Also called vicarious learning. Refers to the extent to which you are acquainted with people who have started successful businesses—either by reading about them or observing them directly. The more you see yourself as similar to these people, the more positive impact knowing them has.
Social Persuasions	The degree to which people encourage or discourage your interest in starting a business directly affects your confidence regarding whether you can do it.
Physiological Factors	How you feel physically when you think about starting your own business. Anxiety and stress lower self-efficacy; excitement and enthusiasm increase it.

J.J. Matis, a successful business owner, affirms the importance of vicarious learning through reading about others. Matis started a company called J.J. Creations which designs, manufactures, and sells a line of backpacks, travel bags, book bags, and similar items primarily for sports fans. In 1999, she looked for something that she could use to carry her water bottle, peanuts, binoculars, and radio when going to a Los Angeles Dodgers game. When she couldn't find anything out of the ordinary, she created a bag herself (she had been sewing since she was a teenager) that looked like a baseball. At the game, she was inundated by people asking her where she got her bag, which prompted her to think that she might be onto a business idea.

She took her idea to Mike Nygren, the merchandising manager for the Dodgers. Nygren encouraged her to make some additional samples and incorporate the project into her MBA program at California Lutheran University. After receiving her MBA, Matis started her business, which took considerable persistence and will. The business now sells bags for a variety of sports teams, politicians, and rock groups. Her "flag-bags" are even featured in the Senate Gift Shop on Capitol Hill in Washington, D.C.

Matis later wrote:

> *"After being a Featured Lady on LadiesWhoLaunch.com in April 2004, I received numerous emails from readers who felt inspired by my story of turning my graduate project into a business. Mostly, their emails expressed how they're planning on starting a business and by reading my story of perseverance and tenacity, they're going ahead with pursuing their ideas for starting a business. It inspires me when people express that I've inspired them!"* [9, 10]

Dealing with Loneliness by Creating a Support Network and Having Faith in Yourself

One thing that surprises many new business owners is that they miss the hectic pace and the busyness of the work environment that they left, where they had frequent interactions with coworkers and others. Many new business owners work alone, especially if they work out of their homes or garages. This type of lifestyle can be lonely, and can be hard to get used to, particularly if you're a "people person" and enjoy frequent interaction with others.

There are at least a couple ways to overcome this challenge. The first is to create a support structure, not just to get business advice, but to have people to interact with and talk to on a regular basis. Brian Magierski, the founder of Kalivo, a company that helps other companies engage with their customers using the latest Internet technologies, said to new business owners:

"It's tremendously rewarding and difficult. You really have to have a sense of purpose about it if you're going to buy into it, because you are generally out on your own. That's part of the appeal of it, but it's also part of what makes it difficult to do as well as frightening to do in some respects. Be prepared for that and create a great support structure behind you whether that's your spouse or your network of friends, because you're going to need it to get through the tough early days."

A second way that business owners can overcome loneliness and prop themselves up is through simple patience, self-confidence, and faith in themselves. These attributes come with maturity and belief in a business idea and are particularly important when not only loneliness, but the exact path the new business will take, is still unclear. Jeff Reifman, the founder of NewsCloud, a social networking site for people interested in news, says:

"I primarily work alone. I have a couple of people I work with, but they're more hourly. These days, I work out of a coffee shop. It's a tough lifestyle. And I think most entrepreneurs who work out of their homes or their garages, they sort of know that early stage.

What's hard about this is when you don't have a model that is ready where you see that there's a plan in front of you, and you're sort of meandering towards experimenting. It's harder to know when that cycle ends. And so, you have to have a lot of faith in yourself, a lot of patience. I say that, as an entrepreneur now as opposed to 10 years ago, I think patience and self-confidence are the qualities that really help me now."[11]

Passion for a Business Idea

A fourth factor that prompts people to start their own businesses is passion for a business idea. What often happens is that a person gets an idea for a new product or service, and there is no practical way to bring the idea to market other than starting a new business. In these instances, a person's willingness to quit her job or start the business part-time often hinges on how passionate he or she is about the product or service idea.

In many cases, a person's passion for a business idea stems from the belief that the idea will positively influence people's lives. This sentiment guided Benjamin Troget, cofounder of Kepner-Tregoe, a management consulting firm. He said:

> *"Tremendously important to me was the feeling that we were doing something that had a significance far beyond building a company or what the financial rewards could be. I was convinced we were doing something that had tremendous importance in the world."*[12]

This level of passion explains why billionaires like Bill Gates of Microsoft, Steven Jobs of Apple, and Larry Page and Sergei Brin of Google continue working after they are financially secure. They strongly believe that the product or service they are selling makes a difference in people's lives and makes the world a better place to live. It also explains why many owner-operated businesses do well in spite of stiff competition. If a business owner is willing to work long hours and commit himself or herself passionately to see a business succeed, that's a combination that's hard to replicate in a regular firm.

An example of the pervasive role of passion in conceiving and launching a new business is provided by John Plaza, the founder of Seattle Biodiesel, a company that makes biodiesel, an environmentally friendly substitute for regular diesel fuel. Plaza, a former airline pilot, quit his job flying commercial airplanes to pursue an interest in alternative fuels. A single flight sparked his passion for environmental stewardship and caused him to decide to make a career change:

> *"I was flying a 747 from Anchorage to Tokyo, and I started thinking about how much fuel that flight used. I figured out that in a 6 hour flight, we used enough fuel to power my personal vehicle for 42 years. I had to make a change."*[13]

The change Plaza made was to start Seattle Biodiesel. To get the business off the ground, Plaza mortgaged his home, sold his boats and cars, and borrowed money against his 401(k). Taking financial actions such as these are common for entrepreneurs who are passionate about their ideas.

How a Father's Attempt to Help His Infant Daughter Through a Health Crisis Ignited Passion for a Business Idea

In 1992, Kenny Kramm's second daughter, Hadley, was born premature. As an infant, she developed a medical disorder that required her to take medicine four times a day. The medicine tasted awful, and Kramm and his wife had a hard time helping Hadley keep it down. The Kramms grew increasingly concerned. Every time Hadley didn't keep down a full dose of the medication, her condition worsened. "We were ending up in the emergency room on a weekly basis," Kramm recalls. While her situation grew more desperate, Hadley's doctors and nurses could do little more than urge the Kramms to help Hadley keep her medicine down—in any way they could.

Kenny Kramm, who worked in his parents' pharmacy, started experimenting with concentrated flavors that could be mixed with Hadley's medicine to mask its bitter taste. Eventually, he and his father produced a banana flavor concentrate that they were able to safely mix with the medicine, and were elated when Hadley started accepting the flavored medicine. Almost immediately, her condition stabilized, both medically and emotionally.

Over the next three years, Kramm and his father continued to experiment with adding flavors to Hadley's various medicines. Gradually, Kramm started seeing his pursuit as a business idea. Surely many other parents faced the same challenge that he and his wife had faced with Hadley, he thought. In 1995, he decided to incorporate and named the business Flavorx. To move the business forward, he partnered with one of the largest flavoring companies in the world to help develop custom flavors that could be safely mixed with medicines. After months of testing, Flavorx's first additives were formally approved.

Flavorx's additives are now available in most pharmacies in the United States and are frequently used to improve the taste of both child and adult medicines. As for Hadley, her father's solution was just what she needed. From the time she took her first dose of banana-flavored medicine, she has never had another medicine-related hospital visit.[14]

The payoff that many business owners receive from their hard work and passion is the level of extreme satisfaction they experience as they work in their businesses every day and watch customers benefit from the products or services they sell. Joy Pierson, the founder of Candle Café and Candle 79, two restaurants in New York City, is such a person. Her restaurants serve organic and vegan food, which provide options to people who not only prefer a certain diet, but have strict dietary restrictions because of allergies or other health concerns. Pierson said her greatest success is...

"...the opportunity to touch people's lives in a profound way through feeding them. We offer menus for people with Celiac disease, who cannot tolerate wheat. One day a child with Celiac disease dined in our restaurant. She was about nine years old and had never been to a restaurant before...she couldn't risk the possibility of cross-contamination from wheat products. She and her family were thrilled that they were able to experience being in a restaurant together to celebrate a special occasion."[15]

A similar example is Lubna Khalid, the founder of Real Cosmetics, a company that creates make-up and skin-care products for women of all nationalities and ethnicities. Khalid started Real Cosmetics as a result of her own personal frustration in not being able to find products and colors for her skin tone. Khalid said:

"What I love about this business is the opportunity to create something new, different, and innovative and the chance to create images and colors that work on a range of skin tones. The other day, we did a photo shoot using seven different models who were women of all different backgrounds. It was incredibly satisfying to produce this shoot and experience the culmination of all my ideas."[16]

One aspect of passion is that it is often used as a proxy by others to determine how committed an individual is to starting a firm and seeing it through. Tom Simpson, an investor who passed on the opportunity to get in on the ground floor of Starbucks because he couldn't see how anyone could make much money selling coffee said, "I missed and completely discounted all the passion that Howard Schultz had and what he was going to set up (and how he planned) to accomplish his goals."[17] Simpson now says that when he meets a team (of prospective business owners), he watches to see if their eyes light up when they make their presentation for funding.

Additional examples of how business owners view passion are shown in Table 1.4.

Table 1.4 The Importance of Passion in Starting New Businesses

Individual and Business Started	View on the Importance of Passion
Jared Ross VENA-Fine Italian Takeout Italian Food Toronto, Canada	My MBA has been invaluable in so many ways. However, one thing business school doesn't teach is how to prepare for the less glamorous, humbling jobs like scrubbing the bathroom floors and driving around the city making deliveries. But it's worth it because I'm **passionate** about my business. For as long as I can remember, I dreamed of being an entrepreneur. Now my dream is a reality, and the risks are mitigated knowing that I reap all the rewards of my hard work. I love every grueling minute of it and can't wait to go to work tomorrow.
Matthew Dunn MusicIP Digital Music Monrovia, California	If you don't have a fundamental "can't walk away from it" **passion** for what you're going to do, you're probably going to have a hard time making it unless you're lucky and even if you do, you'll be tired. I'm never tired of this; I wish there were more hours in the day so that we could do this better and do it faster and do more of it.
Peter Flint Trulia.com Residential Search Engine San Francisco, California	The key is to have a **passion** and to never give up. This is imperative because it creates a drive to solve business problems.

continues

Table 1.4　Continued

Individual and Business Started	View on the Importance of Passion
Judi Sheppard Missett Jazzercise Fitness Franchiser Fitness and Exercise Classes Carlsbad, California	First and foremost, you must be **passionate** about what you're doing—whether you're leading a large group of people through a step class or massaging the kinks out of an individual's body. Out of **passion** develops a strong work ethic, and without it you won't succeed. Some people go into fitness careers thinking, "Oh, it will be a nice thing to do and it will keep me fit." These people don't survive because they don't have enough dedication.
Laura Gasparis Vonfrolio Educational Enterprises Educational Services Richmond, Virginia	The only entrepreneurial trait that is universal, in my view, is **passion**. I've met smart entrepreneurs, stupid entrepreneurs, but they all had **passion**. Some go into it for the fun, some to make money, some to prove a point, some because they don't want to work for anybody else, but the successful ones all have **passion**.
Ross Levin Accredited Investor Edina, Minnesota	You could build a business with anything, as long as you can find something that you can be **passionate** about. If I could have been a minister, I bet I would have built a thriving congregation.

Summary

Ordinary people, just like you, can and do start successful businesses every day. The irony is that many people never get the chance because they think they can't do it or they believe that only extraordinary people start their own businesses. If one or more of the factors that prompt or motivate people to start their own businesses applies to you, you may want to give business ownership more serious consideration.

The next chapter deals with the myth that starting a business involves lots of risk. While there is a measure of risk involved with any endeavor in life, it's important to think about risk holistically. If this chapter has caused you to stop and think,

"Boy, maybe I should do something different with my life. I have unfilled aspirations and passions, too," your biggest risk might be to maintain the status quo, rather than to make the change that will lead to a more satisfying and fulfilling life.

One final note of inspiration. Muhammad Yunus is a Bangladeshi banker who won the Nobel Peace Prize for inventing the concept of microcredit. Microcredit is the extension of small loans to people who can't qualify for traditional financing. Yunus recently wrote a brilliant and heartfelt book titled *Banker to the Poor*. In the book, Yunus took on the myth that it takes an extraordinary person to start a business and also talked about the role of small business (or entrepreneurship) in building economic systems around the world. Yunus wrote:

> "To me, an entrepreneur (small business person) is not an especially gifted person. I rather take the reverse view. I believe that all human beings are potential entrepreneurs. Some of us get the opportunity to express this talent, but many of us never get the chance because we were made to imagine that an entrepreneur is someone enormously gifted and different from ourselves. If all of us started to view every single human being, even the barefooted one begging in the street, as a potential entrepreneur, then we could build an economic system that would allow each man or woman to explore his or her economic potential. The old wall between entrepreneurs and laborers would disappear. It could become a matter of personal choice whether an individual wanted to become an entrepreneur or a wage earner."[18]

Endnotes

1   Murray B. Low and Ian C. MacMillan, "Entrepreneurship: Past Research and Future Challenges," *Journal of Management* 14 (1988): 139–161.

2   Michael McCord, "Career Refilled," Seacoastonline, http://www.seacoastonline.com, 2006 (accessed February 2, 2007).

3   Screenlife home page, http://www.screenlife.com (accessed February 2, 2007).

4   Ladies Who Launch home page, http://www.ladieswholaunch.com (accessed February 5, 2007).

5   Adam Clark, "A Risk Worth Taking," *The Signal*, October 26, 2006, http://www.the-signal.com/ ?module=displaystory&story_id= 33749&format=html (accessed February 6, 2007).

6   Ladies Who Launch.

7   C. Chen, P. Greene, and A. Crick, "Does Entrepreneurial Self-Efficacy Distinguish Entrepreneurs From Managers," *Journal of Business Venturing* 13 (1998): 295–316.

8   Daniel Forbes, "The Effects of Strategic Decision Making on Entrepreneurial Self-Efficacy," *Entrepreneurship Theory and Practice*, September 2005: 599[nd]626.

9   Ladies Who Launch.

10   Ladies Who Launch. Matis's full story, can be accessed by typing her name into the search box.

11   nPost home page, http://www.npost.com (accessed February 5, 2007).

12   Larry C. Farrell, *Entrepreneurial Age: Awakening the Spirit of Enterprise in People, Companies, and Countries* (New York: Allworth Press, 2001).

13   "Seattle Biodiesel Closes $2 Million Financing: New CEO With Package," *Green Car Congress,* July 18, 2005, http://www.greencarcongress.com/2005/07/seattle_biodies.html (accessed February 9, 2007).

14   Flavorx home page, http://www.flavorx.com (accessed February 10, 2007).

15   Ladies Who Launch.

16   Ibid.

17   Monica Soto Ouchi, "Entrepreneurs With Passion Could Hold Secret to Investing Success," *The Seattle Times*, April 19, 2004.

18   Muhammad Yunus, *Banker to the Poor: Micro-Lending and the Battle Against World Poverty* (New York: PublicAffairs, 2003).

Myth No. 2:
Starting a Business Involves
Lots of Risk

Truth No. 2:
It May Not Be as
Risky as You Think

Introduction

If you ask people with traditional jobs why they have never started their own businesses, a very common response you'll get is that starting a business involves too much risk. It's a natural response. In general, people are risk-averse, particularly when it comes to losing something they own or possess. For most of us, there are few things that are more important to our security and sense of self-worth than our jobs. As a result, it's not surprising that people are protective of their jobs and almost instinctively see leaving their jobs to start their own businesses as a risky proposition.

The problem with these sentiments is that they are overly protective and unnecessarily deter people from starting their own businesses. There are many people, some of whom you met in Chapter 1, who have successfully transitioned from traditional jobs to self-employment. The general notion that starting a business involves a great deal of risk is simply not true. The often battered about figure that 9 out of 10 business fail in their first few years is an exaggeration. According to Brian Headd, an economist for the U.S. Small Business Administration, 66% of new businesses are still operating after two years, 50% survive four years or more, and 40% survive six years or more. Additionally, about one-third of all businesses that close or are sold are considered to be successful by their owners.[1]

It's also important to place starting a business as an alternative to traditional employment in its proper perspective. While starting a business involves risk, working for a traditional employer is not risk-free. Between 70,000 and 80,000 corporate employees are laid-off every month, about 30,000 more per month than in the early 2000s. In addition, in many industries, pension funds, health insurance, and other benefits are being trimmed or eliminated at a rapid pace. This is a trend that is occurring in many countries around the world.

A misconception related to the myth that starting a business involves lots of risk is the often expressed sentiment that business owners themselves are risk-seekers. This idea stems largely from the impression that people who start their own businesses are willing to risk their careers, life savings, family relationships, friendships, and emotional well-being on chancy new businesses that might or might not succeed. While starting a business does entail risk, researchers have found that business owners are "moderate" rather than high-risk takers.[2] There are two explanations for this finding. First, rather than plunge blindly into a new venture, business owners tend to take well-informed calculated risks. They also try to accurately discern the degree of risk involved through the techniques we talk about in this chapter. As a result, most business owners don't tend to perceive starting a business as being as risky as you and we might see it. Second, in many cases, business owners redefine the meaning of risk and see their businesses as secondary or acceptable risks in their lives. This scenario played out for Kenny Kramm, the business owner introduced in Chapter 1. Recall, Kramm worked feverishly to find a way to help his infant daughter, Hadley, take her medicine, and as a result, started Flavorx, a company that makes additives that help medicines taste better. For Kramm, the biggest risk in his life was his daughter's health, not the business he was starting. Similar examples include mothers or fathers who start home-based businesses so they can be home with their kids and people who start businesses to pursue passions that are particularly important to them. It's not that these people are reckless or are predisposed to accept higher risks than nonbusiness owners. It's just that they don't see their businesses as high-risk or are willing to accept some additional level of risk, given the other opportunities their businesses allow them to pursue.

If people are in general risk-averse, what type of people, then, are able to set aside the natural tendency to protect their jobs and maintain the status quo and start their own businesses? What set of attributes motivate someone to learn enough about a business opportunity to make a well-informed decision about whether it's a good opportunity or not? Or what set of qualities gives a person sufficient drive to quit her job or work hard enough in her spare time to start a business to accommodate a higher goal, like Kenny Kramm did when he started Flavorx?

Before addressing these issues, we'd like to briefly explain the nature of risk and why it's difficult for people to quit a job to start a business. The very nature of risk inclines people to protect what they have, whether it's a job or another asset, rather than make a dramatic life change like starting a business. After looking at these issues, we'll articulate the attributes that allow people to set aside their aversion to risk and start their own businesses.

Why It's Difficult for People to Quit Their Jobs and Start Their Own Businesses

Risk is a concept that signifies a potential negative impact or outcome that results from a process or future event.[3] In everyday language, we use the term "risk" to indicate the probability of a loss. Two terms that are associated with the study of risk are the *endowment effect* and *loss aversion*. An understanding of both these terms and the concepts behind them provide insight into why it's difficult for people to quit their jobs and start their own businesses.

The endowment effect refers to the fact that people value a good, service, or anything of value more once they posses it.[4] In other words, people place a higher value on things they own opposed to equivalent or even superior items they don't own. In one famous study depicting this effect, college students placed a high value on a coffee mug that had been given to them but put a lower price on a near equivalent mug they did not yet own. There is a very powerful urge among people to protect what they already own or possess, even though something of greater value may be within their reach. It's easy to see how this applies to people and their jobs. When an individual already has a job, his tendency is to protect it, imperfect as it might be, rather than quit that job to start a business. The problem with this tendency is that people often exaggerate the desirability and future potential of a job simply because they have it.

The second dimension of risk that helps explain why it's hard for people to quit their jobs to pursue self-employment is loss aversion, which refers to the tendency for people to strongly prefer avoiding losses rather than acquiring gains.[5] In fact, some studies have shown that losses are as much as twice as psychologically powerful as gains. The way this applies to people and their jobs is similar to the endowment effect. People are reluctant to lose or give up something, like their jobs, even if the possibility exists that they could exchange them for something much better, like different jobs or starting their own businesses. Ironically, what this means is that people often achieve the worst of both worlds without even realizing it. They'll fight hard to keep jobs that are mediocre or poor, simply to avoid losing them, while they are psychologically less inclined to fight hard to gain something that might improve their situations, like different jobs or starting their own businesses.

What "Who Wants to Be a Millionaire?" Teaches Us About Why People Are Reluctant to Start Their Own Businesses

The game show "Who Wants to Be a Millionaire?" is the ideal setting for illustrating the endowment effect and loss aversion. The endowment effect refers to the fact that people value something more once they possess it, while loss aversion refers to the tendency for people to strongly prefer avoiding losses over acquiring gains. Collectively, the two theories help explain why people tend to cling to their present jobs, even if they are sub-par, rather than try to find different jobs or start their own businesses in an effort to improve their situations. It also explains why people on games shows like "Who Wants to Be a Millionaire?" often take the money rather than try for a higher amount.

The way the show works is simple. On a particular show, the host asks a contestant a series of up to 15 questions, each worth a monetary value starting at $100 and moving up to $1 million. For each question the contestant answers correctly, the contestant can either take the money that has been won or risk the money to try to advance to the next level. (The rules varied some during the years of the show.) The game is fun to watch, partly because when a contestant reaches a certain level, like $64,000, either Regis or Meredith (the show's two hosts) shows the contestant a signed check for that amount. This is when the endowment effect and loss aversion often kick in. Once the contestant sees the $64,000 in tangible form, there is a powerful urge to protect and hold onto it, even though much more could be potentially won if the game continues. The effect is even clearer when people preprogram themselves to try to avoid it. This intention is apparent when people say, often with their voices trembling, something like, "I promised myself I would not drop out until I reached the $125,000 question." The reason their voices tremble is because they are fighting a natural urge. Their natural urge is to take the $64,000 and run.

The endowment effect and loss aversion, as they play out in games shows and in everyday life, speak to something that is a deep part of human nature. People are more inclined to go with a sure bet, like taking the $64,000 instead of risking it for a higher amount, or keeping their jobs rather than starting their own businesses, even when they are within an arm's length of significantly more money or a potentially more satisfying career.

In our experience, there are three activities in which people engage to overcome the natural tendency to succumb to the endowment effect and loss aversion and objectively assess whether starting a business is right for them. As you read through and think about these activities, pay particular attention to how each activity can bring clarity and a sense of purposefulness to your life. The problem with succumbing to natural tendencies, like loss aversion and the endowment effect, is that they in effect place a person on autopilot rather than equip them to make more personal and deliberate choices. This outcome can be a good thing when someone reflexively withdraws his or her hand from a hot stove. But it can be a bad thing if it keeps a person in an unsatisfying job when other alternatives, like starting a business, are readily available.

Make an Objective Decision About Starting a Business by Setting Aside Anxieties About Risk

Three activities that can help people transcend loss aversion and the endowment effect to determine whether starting a business is right for them are shown in Figure 2.1. The first two activities, "Determining what you want out of life" and "Having a good sense of what's the 'worst thing that can happen' if your business fails," are usually needed to get a person to the point where he is open to even considering starting his own business.

You'll see this reality reflected in several of the examples that follow. The third activity, "Researching the business opportunity," is needed to help a person assess the attractiveness of a particular business opportunity.

An awareness of these activities can be very helpful for two reasons. First, if you're thinking about starting your own business, the activities can be used as a literal checklist to help you overcome the natural tendency to yield to loss aversion and the endowment effect in your own life. These are powerful effects, and they typically can't simply be willed away. You have to first convince yourself that starting a business is the right thing to do before you can convince others. Second, an awareness of the activities is helpful because, collectively, they are holistic and deal with both the personal and the business side of starting a business.

Let's now take a closer look at these three activities.

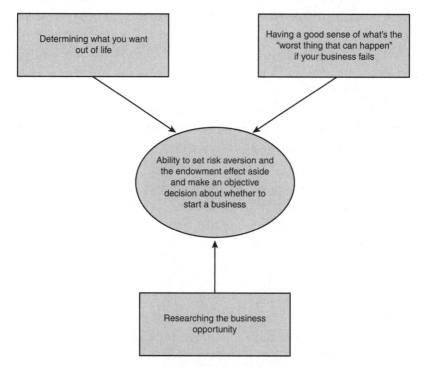

Figure 2.1   *Activities that enable an individual to set aside risk aversion and the endowment effect and make an objective decision regarding whether starting a business is right for him or her*

Determining What You Want Out of Life

The first activity people need to carry out is determining what they want out of life. This is a subjective task that is frequently more difficult than it seems. It is also something people must do for themselves. A mentor, spouse, parent, or book might help a person determine alternatives for her life, but ultimately a person's awareness of what she wants out of her life and career must come from within. Sadly, most people are not vigilant enough about determining what they really want and, as a result, spend precious years in so-so jobs and mediocre lifestyles. An important way of reducing risk in all aspects of life is for a person to determine his most important goals, passions, and aspirations and then focus his valuable time and resources in those areas.

There are many ways to go about gaining an appreciation for what's most important in life. Some people write a personal mission statement or values statement. Others acquire a sense of their most important aspirations and goals more gradually or subtly. Many people also reevaluate what's most important to them as the result of a significant life event, such as the birth of a first child, a health scare, the loss of a job, or a national tragedy like the terrorist attacks on September 11, 2001. These types of events jolt people into thinking through their most important personal goals and priorities.

There are at least two ways that determining what you want out of life can help you set aside risk anxieties and decide whether starting a business is right for you. First, people who have a good sense of what they want out of life tend to look at life holistically and are more likely to select careers or occupations that facilitate the entirety of their lives and aspirations, rather than settling for something that just earns them a paycheck. This is the reason that the vast majority of small businesses are classified as "lifestyle" firms (see Table 1.1). Rather than starting a business to accumulate wealth or gain prestige, the majority of people start businesses to pursue certain lifestyles and make a living at it.

An example of a married couple who started their own business for exactly this reason is Sue Schwaderer and Bill Lawrence. In the late 1990s, Schwaderer was making a six-figure income working for Oracle Software, and Lawrence was successfully managing three apartment buildings they owned in Evanston, Illinois, a Chicago suburb. Although they were making good money, they didn't enjoy their everyday life. "We were tired of never seeing each other and of too much business travel…too much traffic, too many people, too much noise," Schwaderer recalls.[6] The two left their life in Chicago behind and opened up a 14-room bed and breakfast in picturesque Saugatuck, Michigan, a town of 1,000. Although the income from the bed and breakfast doesn't match what they were making in Chicago, they are happier and enjoy the less hectic pace of a smaller town. The desire to pursue what was most important in their life was stronger than the tug of loss aversion and the endowment effect, and they were able to meet their aspirations through business ownership.

Why Two People with Successful Careers Left Their Jobs to Start Their Own Businesses

There is no more vivid an illustration of how having a good sense of what you want out of life can change how you view jobs and careers than when people give up lucrative careers to start businesses that seemingly have much less income potential than the careers they left behind. This is exactly what happened in the cases of Hannah Sullivan and Emily Levy.

Hannah Sullivan spent the majority of her career in high-powered jobs in the investment world. Most recently, she was a general partner at San Francisco-based Fremont Ventures, a part of the Fremont Group, a private investment company that manages more than $10 billion in assets. But her passions have always been hiking, canoeing, and other outdoor activities. In 2001, Sullivan was ready for a break from the investment world. Ironically, about the same time, she met Katie, the owner of Tahoe Trips & Trails (an adventure and travel company), who was ready for a break from her industry. Despite her prestigious career, Sullivan admits that she had been looking into the possibility of either buying or starting an adventure travel company for the previous 10 years. Sullivan quit her job and purchased Tahoe Trips & Trails. She left the investment world and her promising career behind and is now expanding the operations of her new endeavor.

Emily Levy grew up in South Florida helping her mother run a school for students with learning disabilities. She developed an alternative strategy for teaching reading comprehension to dyslexic students, but when it was time for college, she decided to pursue other interests and was accepted into an eight-year medical program at Brown University. Ultimately, Levy deferred medical school to pursue a career in investment banking and money management in New York City.

About a year after she moved to New York, Levy realized that finance wasn't for her but stopped short of quitting her job or going back to medical school. Returning to her true interest and roots, she started tutoring students with learning disabilities part-time.

"Soon my entire after-work schedule was full! I had never worked so hard in my life—doing finance all day and helping kids late into the night," Levy recalls. "I knew I had to make a decision: Stick with a secure job in finance or jump into my real passion."[7]

Levy took the leap and started EBL Coaching, a tutoring service for kids who are struggling in school or trying to overcome learning disabilities.

The second way that determining what you want out of life can help you set aside risk considerations and decide whether starting a business is right for you is if an important aspect of what you want can only be satisfied by starting your own business. This scenario played out for Kimberly Wilson, the founder of Tranquil Space, a yoga studio located in Washington, D.C. Wilson had a successful career as a paralegal but did a lot of yoga in her spare time. She had trouble finding yoga classes that she liked, so she started inviting people to her home to do yoga and provide her own instruction. As her interest in yoga grew, she attended a 200-hour yoga training course in California and made the decision to start her own yoga studio. The transition from working for a company to self-employment was tough, however, and the silent pull of loss aversion and the endowment effect can be felt in Wilson's remembrance of how she felt when she completed her yoga training and returned home to quit her job and start her studio:

> *"I came back from the training and cried. I knew I had to take the plunge, but it was tough to summon the courage. I am thrilled that I did not stick with my comfort zone."*[8]

Another example of how loss aversion and the endowment effect can be overcome if an important aspect of what someone wants can only be satisfied by starting a business is provided by Doug and Lisa Powell. Doug and Lisa, who are both graphic designers, live in the Minneapolis area with their two children. The Powells were a typical family until 2004, when their daughter Maya, who was seven at the time, got sick. It turned out that Maya had type 1 diabetes, a disease that develops in a small percentage of children and young adults. A person with type 1 diabetes has a pancreas that does not produce insulin, a hormone necessary to sustain life. To treat her condition, little Maya would have to prick her finger to test her blood and take insulin one or more times a day for the rest of her life.

As you can imagine, Doug and Lisa Powell initially felt overwhelmed. As the parents of a seven-year-old type 1 diabetic, they needed to quickly learn how to help Maya manage her disease. To accomplish this goal, the Powells set out to try every device available to help Maya understand her condition and to help her cope with her daily regimen. They tried books, alarms, toys, games, medical alert bracelets, and other devices. After trying all these items, they were struck by two things. First, almost everything they found related to type 2 rather than type 1 diabetes. Although "type 1 diabetes" and "type 2 diabetes" sound similar, they are distinctly different diseases. Many of the tools and instructional aids available for type 2 diabetics don't work for people with type 1. The second thing that the Powells noticed was that the vast majority of the material and devices they tried were emotionally cold and intimidating—particularly for a young child. They didn't see how using any of these items could uplift Maya's spirits while teaching her about her disease.

Given what they had discovered, they decided to use their skills as graphic designers to develop their own materials to educate and encourage Maya and help her manage her daily regime. They started sharing the materials with other parents whose children had type 1 diabetes and were surprised by how positive the feedback was. As a result, they decided to start a business, named Type 1 Tools, to share their material and their passion for helping children with type 1 diabetes with other parents and caregivers. Word quickly spread about how effective the Powells' Type 1 Tools are, and people with type 2 diabetes started asking for similar material. The couple obliged and refocused their company, renaming it Type 1 and Type 2 Tools, to help children and adults with both types of diabetes.[9]

Kimberly Wilson and Doug and Lisa Powell all had good jobs and promising careers but developed a keen sense of what was critically important to them in their lives. For Wilson it was starting a yoga studio, and for the Powells it was helping children with type 1 diabetes cope with their disease. In both cases, they couldn't fulfill their most important ambitions through traditional employment or by passing their ideas along to someone else. Starting a business was the only way they could accomplish what was most important to them. They, like other business owners, were able to overcome the natural tendency to avoid risk and start their own businesses by focusing on the more important things in their lives.

Having a Good Sense of What's the "Worst Thing That Can Happen" if Your Business Fails

The second activity or task that helps people set aside loss aversion and the endowment effect and objectively assess whether starting a business is right for them is having a sense of "what's the worst thing that can happen" if the business they're contemplating fails. This activity is not meant to encourage people to be fatalistic, but to develop a reasoned notion of the actual "life risk" involved with starting a particular business. Even if a business endeavor itself is risky, the broader question is how much risk starting the business actually has in the broader scope of a person's life. For example, Michael Dell, who dropped out of college to start Dell Inc., explained, "The opportunity looked so attractive, I couldn't stay in school. The risk was so small. I could lose a year of college."[10]

There are two ways that people frame the issue of "what's the worst thing that can happen if my business fails." The first is to objectively assess the risk of starting the business within the context of their lives. For example, many people start a business part-time before committing to it full-time. In these instances, if the initial results of the business are disappointing, a person can drop the business before she gives up her job. Similarly, in a two-wage-earner household, one spouse can keep his or her job while the other starts a business, and if the spouse that remains in a traditional job is able to cover the family's living expenses, collectively the couple has less risk. This sentiment is affirmed by Manoj Saxena, the founder of Exterprise, a company that helps others build online marketplaces. In response to a question pertaining to the risk involved with starting his business, Saxena said:

> *"Second, I had the financial backing in the form of my wife who was working at IBM and had the ability to support our family. I knew I wouldn't be forced to eat Ramen noodles to survive; we had income coming in that allowed me to focus on Exterprise."*[11]

There are other types of businesses that objectively have little risk. Examples include home-based eBay businesses and direct-sales businesses, like Tupperware and May Kay, where the upfront investment is relatively low. Many people who are otherwise risk-averse have no problem starting these types of businesses because the business can essentially be suspended at any time with little or no cost. Other people lower the risk associated with their businesses by relying strictly on their own funds and operating in a very frugal manner.

The second way people frame the issue of "what's the worse thing that can happen if my business fails" is to fix in their minds a fall-back position if their businesses fail. This sentiment is often prevalent in people who have skills that are in high demand, like engineering or computer programming, and intuitively know that if they leave their employer on good terms to start a business, and the business fails, they will have little trouble reentering the work-force. This type of outlook is also prevalent among younger people who see their whole lives ahead of them and aren't afraid of starting over if a business endeavor fails. This view is expressed by Joyce Rita Hazan, the founder of Rita Hazan Salon. When asked about the risk involved with her business, Hazan said:

> *"I didn't think about it [being a risk]. I thought, 'What's the worse thing that can happen?' So I lose everything, and I can move in with my mom. What do I have to lose? Money? Big deal. I can make that again. I'll still have a roof over my head and people who love me."*[12]

Researching the Business Opportunity

The third activity or task that helps people set loss aversion and the endowment effect aside and objectively assess whether starting a business is right for them is researching the specific business opportunities they are considering. Taking time to learn the ins and outs of an opportunity is largely what makes business owners moderate rather than high-risk takers. The most common way to reduce anxiety in any facet of life is to collect information and become well-informed. It is also one of the most common forms of advice given to prospective business owners. "If you're ready to take the risk of starting a new enterprise, research your business carefully before taking the plunge," says Tony Lee, an editor for StartupJournal, the *Wall Street Journal's* Web site for small business. "Even though business failure rates aren't as high as we think, aspiring entrepreneurs need to do their homework."[13] Similar words of advice are provided by Stephen Light, the founder of Flow Corp, a company that makes high pressure water cutting machines. "Before you launch a new service, you do everything you can to understand it and try to mitigate the risk surrounding it."[14]

In our experience, there are three primary ways that prospective business owners successfully approach the task of researching a particular business opportunity:

1. Get advice from experts and informed people.
2. Gather general information about an opportunity.
3. Write a business plan.

Candidly, our experience has taught us that people who frequently kick around the idea of starting their own businesses but never actually do are often guilty of engaging in none of these activities. Again, one of the primary reasons that business owners don't tend to perceive starting a business as being as risky as the general public might see it is that they have studied the process and have an informed awareness of the potential risks and rewards involved.

The first approach that prospective business owners often take to research an opportunity is to talk to informed people about the opportunity/industry they are thinking about entering. People often surprise themselves by the quality of feedback and advice they are able to obtain from industry leaders and other informed individuals simply by asking for help. This point is affirmed by Larry Smith, the founder of *SMITH* magazine, which features amazing stories about ordinary people. When asked what advice he would give to aspiring business owners, Smith replied:

> *"Don't be afraid to ask for help. I learned that 9 times out of 10 people are usually nice. I just went to people and said, 'Hey, I'm working on this new magazine, and could I speak with you about it.' People are amazing! I went to the editors of* ReadyMade *(a magazine for people who like to make things), and they could've easily looked at me as a competitor. Instead, they just laid it out for me. I wasn't afraid to cold call anybody, and it just amazed me how fantastic and helpful people can be. What's the worst they can do? Say no!"*[15]

Another approach prospective business owners use to collect information and reduce their anxieties about a particular opportunity is to ask people who are in the business or industry about their experiences. This approach was pursued by Carleen

Peaper, the owner of a Cruise Planners franchise. Prior to buying the franchise, Peaper contacted a number of current Cruise Planner franchisees to see what their experiences had been:

> *"I was really apprehensive about making an investment of my time and money into a franchise, so I e-mailed 50 Cruise Planner agents with a set of questions, asking for honest feedback. Everyone responded. That was a big thing that helped me determine that I wanted to join them. I also liked the way the company runs. They give us support, training, and tools but let us run with it. You can work with big groups, luxury travel, or whatever fits you."*[16]

This type of feedback is invaluable. It not only provided Peaper a sense of the level of satisfaction that Cruise Planner franchisees have, but provided her additional information about the way the company operates.

The second way that prospective business owners conduct research is to study industry (or business-specific) books, magazines, Web sites, and databases. If you don't know where to start this type of pursuit, a good place to begin is by visiting a college, university, or large public library. Simply approach a reference librarian and say, "I am thinking about starting a business in the cruise industry (or whatever industry you are interested in), can you direct me to information that might be helpful to me?" Often, a wealth of insightful information will flow from this type of inquiry.

Starting to Research a Business Idea: Begin Your Search at a College, University, or Public Library

In the age of Google and Yahoo!, it's easy to confine the research we complete on a topic to Internet searches. But one of the most frequently overlooked and valuable places to start investigating the merits of a business opportunity is at a library. Large public or university libraries have accesses to magazines, trade journals, and databases, which would cost hundreds if not thousands of dollars to access from home. A skilled librarian can use a database like ReferenceUSA, for example, to find the number of pet stores in Lincoln, Nebraska, where the stores are located in the city, and what the average income is in the neighborhoods surrounding each of the stores. Imagine how useful this type of information would be to someone putting together a business plan on opening a pet store in Lincoln. Along with providing access to the information, the typical reference librarians will also spend time with individuals to show them how the databases work and how queries are conducted. Some librarians will even put together a market research study on behalf of a prospective business owner for a nominal or very reasonable fee.

To promote business startups in a city or region, many libraries now offer expanded services to people thinking about starting their own businesses. The services often include classes, networking opportunities, and access to business professionals to solicit advice from. In fact, since it opened 10 years ago, the Science, Industry and Business Library, which is part of the New York Public Library in Manhattan, says it has trained 64,000 people through its 20 free classes. Examples of courses offered in a recent session included the following:

- Introduction to Patents

- Companies & Contacts: Creating Customized Lists

- Research 101: The Basics

- Research 102: Getting the Most out of Online Databases

Another common service offered by libraries is to provide office space for SCORE (Service Corp of Retired Executives) volunteers to meet with prospective business owners. SCORE volunteers provide free advice to prospective business owners on a wide range of business topics, including how to identify a target market, how to put together a marketing plan, how to set up an accounting system, and how to obtain a business license.

Other strategies for conducting business research include reading industry trade journals (which can be easily identified through an Internet search) and industry-specific magazines and by studying the Web sites of potential competitors. Attending industry trade shows is also a good strategy. Also reading business magazines geared toward small businesses, like *Fortune Small Business, Inc.*, and *Entrepreneur*, can provide invaluable insight and information. Reading these types of publications is also a confidence builder. As shared in Chapter 1, the more people in traditional jobs read and learn about business owners, the more they come to realize that owning and running a business is well within the reach of most individuals.

The third way that prospective business owners conduct research in an effort to learn more about a business opportunity and overcome risk anxieties is to write a *business plan*. A business plan is a written document that carefully explains every aspect of a new business venture. In many instances, having a business plan is a sheer necessity. Most bankers and investors, for example, won't consider financing a business that doesn't have a formal business plan.

Publications on how to write a business plan are available at bookstores like Borders and Barnes & Noble and local Small Business Development Centers, and SCORE chapters often sponsor workshops on how to write a business plan. Most business plan are between 20 and 30 pages long and follow a conventional format outlined in the books and taught through the workshops. Although writing a business plan may appear at first glance to be a tedious process, a properly prepared business plan can save a business owner a tremendous amount of time, money, and heartache by working out the kinks in a business idea and by providing a firm understanding of the risk involved before rather than after the business is started.

Writing a business plan is not a trivial event. A well-conceived plan normally takes several days or weeks to prepare. The upside is that for someone who is serious about a particular business opportunity, writing a business plan will reveal more about the potential risks and rewards involved than any other single activity. If the plan reveals to a prospective business owner that there is too much risk surrounding a particular business opportunity, reaching that conclusion should be considered to be a successful outcome of the business planning process. It is better to fail on paper than for real. Conversely, the plan might reassure a prospective business owner that the business idea is viable and has a high probability of succeeding. This type of conclusion would help a prospective owner set aside loss aversion and the endowment effect and move forward in pursuing the business opportunity.

Summary

The primary message of this chapter is that people are in general risk-averse and must take purposeful steps to overcome their natural tendency toward loss aversion before they are able to quit their jobs and start their own businesses. This set of circumstances is not necessarily a bad thing. You should feel good about the risks involved with a particular business opportunity and your ability to manage the risks before you leave a stable job to start your own business. But an equally important message conveyed by the chapter is that people often exaggerate how good their present jobs or careers are simply because they have them. This tendency causes people to unnecessarily limit themselves in visualizing the options possible for their lives.

The next chapter deals with the amount of money it takes to start a successful business. We hope you find the chapter to be a breath of fresh air. Many businesses are started for much less money than you might think. We'll help you organize your thinking about the role of money in the start-up process.

Endnotes

[1] B. Headd, "Redefining Business Success: Distinguishing Between Closure and Failure," *Small Business Economics* 21 (2003): 51–61.

[2] R. Brockhaus, "Risk Taking Propensity of Entrepreneur," *Academy of Management Journal* 23:3 (1980): 509–520.

[3] Wikipedia, http://www.wikipedia.org (accessed March 11, 2007).

[4] Ibid.

[5] Ibid.

[6] M. Henricks, "Freedom, Not Money, Drives These Startups," *The Wall Street Journal*, May 29, 2002.

[7] Ladies Who Launch, accessed March 12, 2007 (see chap. 1, n. 4).

[8] Ibid.

[9] Type 1 and Type 2 Tools home page, http://www.type1tools.com (accessed March 10, 2007).

[10] Jeremy Main, "A Golden Age for Entrepreneurs," *Fortune*, February 12, 1990: 120.

[11] nPost, accessed March 10, 2007 (see chap. 1, n. 11).

[12] Ladies Who Launch, accessed March 12, 2007 (see chap. 1, n. 4).

[13] SCORE home page, http://www.sloscore.org (accessed March 12, 2007).

[14] nPost, accessed March 12, 2007 (see chap. 1, n. 11).

[15] "Being My Boss—Larry Smith," StyleStation blog, http://stylestation.typepad.com (accessed March 12, 2007).

[16] Julie Bennett, "Cruise Franchisee Says It's Been Smooth Sailing," *Startup Journal*, www.startup.wsj.com, http://online.wsj.com/article/S60223BENNETT.html?mod=RSS_Startup_Journal&sjrss=frontpage (accessed March 2, 2007).

Myth No. 3:
It Takes a Lot of Money to
Start a Business

Truth No. 3:
It Might Not Cost as
Much as You Think

How much do you think it costs to start a business? If you're thinking about a biotechnology, semiconductor, or medical product firm, you'd probably say a lot, and you'd be right. But how much do you think it costs to start an average business, like the privately owned businesses you deal with every day? And where do you think the majority of the start-up capital for these businesses comes from? According to the *Wells Fargo/Gallup Small Business Index*, the average small business is started for about $10,000, with the majority of the money coming from the owners' personal savings.[1]

If this figure strikes you as low, you're in good company; it strikes most people as low. That's because when most people think of businesses, they think of the types of businesses that they interact with the most frequently, like grocery stores, restaurants, gas stations, and large retail stores. These types of business do take a lot of money to start and run. But chances are if you start a business, it won't be like these businesses—at least initially. It will be more like the businesses highlighted so far in this book. Most of these businesses didn't take a tremendous amount of money to start. Even aggressive growth firms, in most cases, don't take an arm and a leg to get started. Each year *Inc.* magazine compiles a list of the 5,000 fastest-growing privately owned firms in the United States. In 2006, the medium amount it took to start one of the businesses on the list was $75,000.[2] That means that half of them were started for less than $75,000. And these firms cover a wide swath of businesses, from building contractors to advertising agencies to retail stores.

There is somewhat of a catch, however, involved with starting a business with limited funds. The catch is that most people simply don't have any experience or insight when it comes to determining how much it will cost to start a business, how to economize on start-up expenses, or how to raise money if needed. These are topics that there is no reason to think about until you start seriously thinking about starting a business. To provide insight regarding these issues and to further dispel the myth that it takes a lot of money to start a business, this chapter is divided into three sections. The first section provides insights into how to think about money as it relates to starting a business. The second section focuses on the techniques that enable business owners to minimize the costs associated with starting a business. The third section focuses on the choices that small business owners have for raising start-up funds if needed.

Insights Into How to Think About Money as It Relates to Starting a Business

For most people, the topic that consumes the majority of their thinking as it relates to money and starting a specific business is "How much money will it take to get the business off the ground?" While this question makes perfect sense, there is no concrete answer. The same exact business might cost one person $10,000 to start and another person $25,000—trust us, this isn't an exaggeration. The amount needed typically depends on how a person thinks about money as it relates to starting a business, how frugal a person is, and how resourceful a person is in gaining access to money and other resources.

While money is obviously needed to start even the most basic business, many of the observations that successful business owners make about money are surprising. While you'd think money would be held in high esteem, many business owners discount the importance of having plentiful funds as a key to new business success. Instead, they tend to see the absence of money as a motivator for developing qualities such as resourcefulness, creativity, focus, frugality, and drive.

The following are three insights about the role of money in the start-up process. As you read through each insight, think carefully about how each topic relates to your own attitudes about money. One of the reasons that many businesses are started for as little money as they are is that people adjust their attitudes about money as they become more acquainted with the start-up process.

Now let's look at three insights regarding the role of money in the start-up process.

Skimpy Finances Can Be a Blessing Rather Than a Curse

The first insight regarding money and the start-up process is that there is a silver lining to having limited start-up funds. Many successful business owners, when they reflect back on their start-up years, feel that having limited funds forced them to focus, become self-reliant, and develop a mindset of frugality—qualities that have served them well as they've grown their firms.

The importance of focus is affirmed by Caterina Fake, cofounder of Flickr, the popular photo-sharing Web site, which was started in 2002. In reflecting back on the role of money in the early days of her firm, Fake said:

> *"The money was scarce, but I'm a big believer that constraints inspire creativity. The less money you have, the fewer people and resources you have, the more creative you have to become. I think that had a lot to do with why we were able to iterate and innovate so fast."*[3]

Flickr's first product was a multiplayer online game called Game Neverending. At one point mid-way through the development of the game, the programmers, on a lark, added an instant messenger application to the game's environment, which allowed users to form communities to share photos. Surprisingly, the photo-sharing feature quickly passed the game itself in terms of popularity. As the photo-sharing feature continued to gain momentum, the game itself was dropped because the company couldn't afford to work on both projects simultaneously. Flickr (www.flickr.com), as a photo-sharing Web site, became extremely popular and was acquired by Yahoo! in 2005 for somewhere between 20 and 30 million dollars. Ironically, it was the lack of money, rather than the abundance of it, that caused the founders of Flickr to drop the game and focus on the photo-sharing site, a decision that turned out to be very profitable for the company.

In regard to developing a culture of self-reliance, having limited start-up funds often instills discipline in a firm and forces the founders to substitute ingenuity and hard work for financial resources. An example of how this played out in one firm is provided by Doris Christopher, the founder of The Pampered Chef. Christopher started The Pampered Chef in 1980 and ran the company out of her home well beyond its start-up years. Explaining how having limited start-up funds helped set her on a lifelong track of financial discipline, Christopher wrote:

> *"With a bankroll of only $3,000 to start my business, I didn't have any choice; I had to watch my overhead. It taught me discipline, which I have been mindful of throughout my business career."*[4]

The Pampered Chef, which was started in 1980, has been an enormously successful company. It sells kitchen utensils through home parties, utilizing a direct sales approach (like Tupperware). At last count, the company had nearly 70,000 Pampered Chef consultants and 12 million people attending its home parties each year. To this day, the main theme of Christopher's speaking and writing is to caution business owners to avoid debt, minimize overhead, and remain self-reliant.

Finally, limited funds at the outset often help a firm develop a mindset of frugality—a quality that is often very helpful as a firm grows and expands. For example, many businesses that are started on a shoestring learn to function very inexpensively and continue to watch their money very carefully, even after they become successful.

How Not Having Much Money Helped One Founding Team Learn to Be Self-Reliant and Receive a Nice Payoff When Its Business Was Acquired

In the early 1990s, Ron Gruner, a serial entrepreneur, launched Shareholder.com, a company that helped large firms better communicate with their shareholders. The company started with no investment capital and funded its growth entirely through earnings. There were times, Gruner readily admits, when having more money would have been nice and would have enabled the firm to grow much faster. But the benefit of having limited funds was that the company became self-reliant, and its employees learned how to substitute ingenuity and hard work for money. In an interview Gruner gave to Jessica Livingston, the author of *Founders at Work*, he recalled a specific example that makes this point:

"Here's an example: Back when the whole Internet thing was getting started, I hired a computer consultant to come in and advise us about what our Internet infrastructure should be. He was a well-credentialed, Microsoft-accredited engineer, etc. He came in and said, 'You need to buy x number of servers and this kind of software and all that, and it's a quarter of million dollars to do it right.' We said we couldn't even come close to doing that. So I went down to Barnes & Noble, bought several books, including some of the Dummy series. And we built our first Internet servers, which lasted us several years, on Gateway desktop computers, using Microsoft Access as our database system and using basically off-the-shelf server software. We did that for $3 [thousand] or 4,000, and it worked great."[5]

This type of behavior—doing things yourself rather than spending a lot of money—is referred to as bootstrapping, a practice we'll talk about later in the chapter. In Shareholder.com's case, an added benefit of learning to be self-reliant was that it motivated the company to remain independent during the heady dot-com era of the late 1990s and early 2000s, when money from investors was readily available. By not taking money, the company was able to remain nimble and react quickly to competitive challenges because it didn't have to consult with bankers or investors before it made a decision.

Shareholder.com grew steadily through the years, and the payoff came in 2006 when the firm was acquired by NASDAQ. Because Gruner and his team learned to be self-reliant and live with limited funds, they didn't have anyone to split the proceeds with when the firm was sold.

Raising or Borrowing Money Is Trading One Boss for Another

The second insight regarding the role of money and the start-up process has to do with raising equity capital or borrowing to fund a business. One of the first things that many people do when they decide to start a business is to try to raise money through a bank or an investor. There are several choices that business owners have for raising money, including commercial banks, SBA guaranteed loans, investors, grants, supplier financing, and several others. Of these choices, many people automatically assume that the only way they'll raise the amount of money they need is via a commercial bank or an equity investor. While the other choices might hold promise, most people's initial reactions are that the alternatives pale in comparison to the amount of money that can be raised from a bank or through an investor.

While in some cases it is necessary to go the bank or investor route, the problem with obtaining money from these sources is that there are consequences that business owners often don't fully anticipate. Bankers and investors typically assert considerable control over the businesses they provide money to as a means of protecting their investments. While the majority of bankers and investors have good intentions, the level of scrutiny and control their investments allow them often has an impact on the firms they fund. For example, banks are inherently conservative and often caution their clients to grow slowly, while investors are the opposite and regularly pressure the companies they invest in to grow quickly to increase their valuations. What's missing here is what the business owner wants. So for people leaving traditional jobs to start their own businesses, obtaining money from bankers or investors is often like trading one boss for another. You might be freeing yourself from working for a boss in a traditional sense but could have an equally influential boss in the form of a banker or an investor.

An additional consideration when taking money from an investor is that you exchange partial ownership in your business for funding. This aspect of the small business owner–investor relationship can also be problematic. Unlike the business owners introduced in this book, who started their businesses to fulfill personal aspirations or follow their passions, the majority of investors are not in it for the long term—they want their money back in three to five years along with a sizeable return. This means that a business owner like Daryn Kagan, the former CNN reporter who started a "good news" Web cast, will probably have to sell her business in three to five years from the time it was started if she accepted investment capital. Although this scenario will undoubtedly net Ms. Kagan a handsome financial return, assuming her business is gaining traction and is profitable, she'll lose direct control of the business she was so excited to create.

The solution to avoid these potential problems is steering clear of bank financing or equity funding or, at the minimum, having a clear understanding of the nature of the relationship you'll have with your banker or investors. It's possible for a small business owner to have a healthy relationship with a banker or an investor. The overarching point, however, is that small business owners should go into these relationships with their eyes wide open, fully understanding the parameters of the relationships they're developing.

Excess Funds Can Enable a start-up to Operate Unprofitably for Too Long

The third insight regarding money and the start-up process is that having excess funds often masks problems and enables a firm to operate unprofitably for too long. Many businesses lose money their first several months while they ramp up and gain customers. That's normal. But at some point, a business has to operate profitably to prove that it is a viable, ongoing pursuit. People who start businesses with limited funds typically find out quickly if their businesses are capable of turning a profit. Because they don't have excess funds to rely on, they must make adjustments quickly, like cutting expenses or increasing sales, to turn a profit. Ultimately, if the business doesn't work, it is shut down. In contrast, if a person starts a business with abundant funds, the business can operate for months at a loss and stay open if the owner relies on excess funds to keep the business afloat. The owner may never feel pressured to cut costs or generate additional sales, thinking that the business simply needs more time to prove itself. If the business ultimately fails, it will normally lose more money and more of its owner's time and prestige than the less well funded startup.

A related complication associated with having abundant funds is that a business's cost structure and clientele is often determined by the amount of money it has initially. For example, if you decided to open a clothing store and were offered $200,000 by an investor to start the business, you might rent space in an upscale mall, hire experienced salespeople, buy the latest computer equipment, and launch an expensive advertising campaign. While this sounds good, once the business is started and the $200,000 is gone, you might be locked into a high overhead business that has to sell high margin products to an affluent clientele to make the business work. Conversely, if you had started with less money, you might have signed a shorter tem lease in a more modest facility, hired your initial salespeople part-time to see which ones worked out the best, bought used computer equipment, and found inexpensive ways to spread the word about your store. Utilizing this approach, you'd actually have more flexibility and room to maneuver than the better funded scenario.

Collectively, the purpose of these three insights is to put the importance of money in starting a business in its proper perspective. While many people think, "If I only had the money, I'd start my own business," the insights provided here show that having money isn't a panacea. In fact, the discipline imposed by having limited funds is often an advantage and creates a healthier business in the long run.

The next section of this chapter focuses on techniques that enable business owners to minimize the costs associated with starting up. While many businesses ultimately do need to raise some money to get started, the amount needed can be greatly reduced through creative and novel cost-cutting techniques.

Techniques That Enable Business Owners to Minimize the Costs Associated with Starting a Business

As mentioned earlier in the chapter, the numbers reported for the average cost of starting a business strike most people as low. When you think about the cost of buying a car or even a major household appliance, it's easy to question whether the average business is really started for around $10,000. The answer is that while it might cost $10,000 to start the average business, that figure doesn't tell the whole story. Many business owners put a tremendous amount of free labor into starting their firms and become experts at scraping and scrounging to gain access to resources at reduced cost. In fact, many observers believe that a business owner's ability to "bootstrap" all or part of its resource needs is a key to business success. The term *bootstrap* comes from the German legend of Baron Munchausen pulling himself out of the sea by pulling on his own bootstraps. In start-up circles, bootstrapping means finding ways to avoid the need for bank financing or investor funding through creativity, ingenuity, thriftiness, cost-cutting, or any means necessary.[6]

This section of the chapter focuses on three techniques that enable business owners to minimize the costs associated with starting a business. The techniques include selecting an appropriate business to start, seeking help, and cutting costs and saving money at every available opportunity.

Selecting an Appropriate Business to Start

The first step involved in minimizing the costs associated with starting a business is to select an appropriate business. If you have limited funds, you should start a business that requires a small up-front investment, has a short sales cycle (meaning the customer decides quickly whether to buy), has short repayment terms (30 days or less), and has a high degree of recurring revenue. Businesses with the opposite characteristics generally take too much money for a business owner with limited resources to start and run.

Fortunately, there are many businesses that meet the criteria described. Home-based businesses, which now represent more than half of the 26.8 million U.S. small businesses, are popular largely because they take very little capital to start and have low overhead. The cost savings that are realized by operating a home-based business often help these businesses earn profits from the start, which helps them accumulate the funds necessary to move into larger quarters when needed. This is exactly what happened in the case of Emily Levy, the founder of EBL Coaching, the tutoring service for children introduced in Chapter 2. Commenting on her start-up experience, Levy wrote:

> *"My start-up costs were minimal since I was working out of my apartment. Now that the business has grown, however, I have to pay for office space, insurance, advertising and tutors, but EBL Coaching has been profitable from the start. There are many businesses that you can start with minimal capital, especially if you start small and grow organically as demand increases."*[7]

Service businesses are also fairly inexpensive to start depending on the nature of the business. Though not exhaustive, a list of service businesses that typically meet the criteria discussed above are shown in Table 3.1. An example from the table is a home inspector. Nearly every real estate transaction requires a home inspection, making it a fairly lucrative business. The up-front costs of becoming a home inspector are fairly modest, which include training and certification and a basic set of home inspection tools. The sales cycle is short, considering that once an inspection is ordered, it is normally completed within a few days. The repayment term is also short because the inspector usually requires payment the day of the inspection. And there is normally a high degree of recurring revenue. Even though the same people don't normally require repeat inspections, the vast majority of a home inspector's business comes from referrals from builders and real estate agents.

Table 3.1   Examples of Service Businesses That Are Attractive Alternatives for Prospective Business Owners with Limited Funds

Automotive Detailing	Massage Therapist
Bookkeeper	Messenger Service
Bridal Consultant	Nanny Service
Career Counselor	Online Retailer
Counselor/Psychologist	Photographer
Daycare Service	Property Management Service
eBay Store	Public Relations Consultant
Executive Search Firm	Tax Preparation Service
Financial Planner	Transcription Service
Home Inspector	Travel Agent
Interior Designer	Tutoring Service

The types of businesses that aren't good choices for prospective business owners with limited funds are businesses that bring new products to market, businesses that are capital-intensive like manufacturing firms, and businesses that require a lot of employees like a call center. While these businesses might have more potential profitability than home-based businesses and service firms, they simply take too much money to start for someone with limited start-up funds.

Seek Out Help

The second technique that helps business owners minimize the costs associated with starting a business is to seek out coaching and assistance. There are many ways for new businesses to get this type of help. The Small Business Development Center (SBDC), for example, is a government agency that provides free management assistance and coaching to small business owners. Your local SBDC can be identified at www.sba.gov/sbdc. Another good choice is the Service Corps of Retired Executives (SCORE), which is a nonprofit organization that provides free consulting services to small businesses. SCORE's 10,000+ volunteers are retired business owners who counsel in areas as diverse as finance, operations, ecommerce, and sales. You can find your local SCORE chapter at www.score.org. Both of these organizations can provide business owners concrete advice and suggestions for how to minimize the costs of starting a specific business.

Prospective business owners should also identify local small business and entrepreneurship organizations to plug into. These organizations offer seminars, sponsor networking events, hold business plan competitions, and introduce their members to service providers and potential sources of financing or funding. An example is the Oregon Entrepreneurs Network (www.oen.org), an organization that services prospective business owners in Oregon and southwest Washington. The organization, which charges a nominal membership fee, provides its members a full slate of programs and services. A similar example is the Venture Lab at the University of Central Florida in Orlando, Florida (www.venture-lab.ucf.edu). The Venture Lab provides coaching and advice to anyone in Central Florida who has a business idea and needs help assessing the merits of the idea and shaping it into a viable business. There are similar organizations in almost every city in the United States.

Finally, there are organizations that provide coaching, advice, and support to specific groups of business owners and tailor their offerings to fit the groups. An example is Ladies Who Launch (www.ladieswholaunch.com), an organization that sponsors workshops and provides materials that encourage and support female business owners. The workshops include discussions, case studies, stories, and anecdotes that help women leverage their unique abilities to launch businesses efficiently and effectively. Similar organizations and support groups are available for veterans, members of minority groups, college students, senior adults, and other demographic groups.

Cut Costs and Save Money at Every Opportunity

The most obvious way to minimize the costs associated with launching a business is to cut costs and save money at every opportunity. The most effective way to do this is to develop a mindset of frugality and resourcefulness. While these attributes might seem obvious, in many cases, frugality and resourcefulness are learned skills. Many people aren't naturally frugal or resourceful, but as a result of an intensive desire to make their businesses work, they foster these qualities to help get their businesses off the ground and to minimize the costs of their ongoing operations.

A list of common cost-cutting and cost-saving techniques is provided below. While the techniques are well known, the trick is to put them into action. An example of a business owner who put the third item on the list, "Look for opportunities to barter," is provided by Clara Rankin Williams, the founder of Clara Belle Collections, a jewelry design business. When asked for words of advice regarding how to start and run a business, Williams said:

> *"Take advantage of random situations. I was at a truck show and I heard a friend talking with a marketing consultant. I asked the consultant whether there was any chance she might be interested in helping me with my marketing and swapping jewelry for services. She was. As an entrepreneur, you have to think out of the box, especially if you want to survive in an increasingly crowded marketplace."*[8]

This type of behavior exemplifies a mindset of frugality and resourcefulness. There are other cost-cutting and cost-saving techniques that aren't as well known as those shown in the following bulleted list. A sample of these techniques includes employing open source software instead of more expensive proprietary software packages, writing or participating in blogs as an alternative to buying advertising, utilizing online tools such as Skype instead of paying for long distance, and eliminating the cost of buying a fax machine by utilizing an online fax forwarding service such as eFax.

- Buy used instead of new equipment.
- Coordinate purchases with other businesses.
- Barter.
- Lease equipment rather than buying.
- Obtain payments in advance from customers.
- Minimize personal expenses.
- Avoid unnecessary expenses, such as lavish office space or furniture.
- Buy items cheaply but prudently through discount outlets or online auctions such as eBay, rather than at full-price stores.

There are many examples of business owners who dramatically reduced the cost of launching their businesses by utilizing combinations of the techniques described here. One example is provided by Michelle Madhok, the founder of SheFinds (www.shefinds.com), a company that helps people find bargains on the Internet:

> *"I financed SheFinds myself and have spent about $5,000 of my own money to get the business off the ground. The most expensive items were forming the LLC [which is a form of business ownership], legal costs, and public relations. My [Web] site was built for about $250 by a guy in the Ukraine who I found on Craig's List (www.craigslist.com). My photos were done for barter, and I got a good deal on the illustrations on my site because the artist had downtime. I worked with many independents—my lawyer was an independent, because I [didn't] see the value in paying for a big, fancy firm. And I looked for discount resources on the Internet—if you search around, you can find companies that will make quality color copies for about 20 cents a copy."[9]*

Madhok's experience is a clear example of a firm that cost $5,000 to start but could easily have cost $25,000 absent her frugal mindset and deliberate attempts to cut costs.

Choices That Small Business Owners Have for Raising Start-Up Funds if Needed

Some startups do need to raise money to get their businesses off the ground. In these instances, it's been our experience that the most knowledgeable and well-informed business owners have the most success. The most common mistake that prospective business owners make is not having a business plan. Although some books and magazine articles suggest that a business plan isn't necessary, our experience has taught us that this advice is dead wrong. It's almost inconceivable that a business would be successful obtaining money from a bank, an investor, a granting agency, a supplier, or future customer without a business plan that describes the business and validates its financial potential. Help for writing a business plan can be obtained from the SBDC, SCORE, or other small business support groups. There are also books detailing how to write a business plan available at Borders, Barnes & Noble, and Amazon.com. The first author of this book has a business plan book titled *Preparing Effective Business Plans: An Entrepreneurial Approach*, which can be obtained via Amazon.com or a similar online bookstore.

A second mistake people often make when looking for financing or funding is that they don't cast their nets wide enough. There are many sources of financing and funding available for small businesses. As a result, it is poor strategy to place too much reliance on some sources of funding and not enough on others.

This section of the chapter outlines the choices that small business owners have for raising start-up funds if needed. The alternatives include bank financing, equity funding, grants, and a few others.

Bank Financing

Historically, commercial banks have not been a practical source of financing for start-up firms. Most banks are relatively conservative and won't loan money to a business that doesn't have a proven track record and some type of collateral. That's not to say that you can't get a home equity loan to fund part or all of the money you need. It's just that most banks won't assume the risk of loaning money directly to a business with an unproven track record. They would rather loan money to an individual who has equity in a home to pledge as collateral.

The Small Business Administration (SBA) Guaranteed Loan Program is a realistic alternative for many business startups. The SBA does not have money to lend but makes it easier for business owners to obtain loans from banks by guaranteeing the loans. Approximately 50% of the 9,000 commercial banks in the United States participate in the Guaranteed Loan Program. The most notable SBA program available to small businesses is the 7(A) Loan Guaranty Program. The loans are for small businesses that are not able to obtain loans on reasonable terms through normal lending channels. Almost all small businesses are eligible to apply for an SBA guaranteed loan. The SBA can guarantee as much as 85% (debt to equity) on loans up to $150,000 and 75% on loans over $150,000. In most cases, the maximum guarantee is $1.5 million. A guaranteed loan can be used for working capital to start a new business or expand an existing one. It can also be used for real estate purchases, renovation, construction, or equipment purchases. The best way to learn more about the SBA Guaranteed Loan Program and determine if you are eligible is to meet with a participating lender.

There are a variety of other avenues that business owners can pursue to borrow money. Credit cards should be used with extreme caution. One channel for borrowing funds that is getting quite a bit of attention is Prosper (www.prosper.com), a peer-to-peer lending network. Prosper is an online auction Web site that matches people who want to borrow money with people who are willing to make loans. Most of the loans made via Prosper are fairly small ($25,000 or less) but might be sufficient to meet a new business's needs. There are also organizations that lend money to specific demographic groups. For example, Count Me In (www.countmein.org), an advocacy group for female business owners, provides loans of $500 to $10,000 to women starting or growing a business. An organization that is aligned with Count Me In and American Express, named Make Mine a Million $ Business (www.makemineamillion.org), lends up to $45,000 strictly to female-owned startups.

There are also lenders who specialize in "microfinancing" which are very small loans. For example, Accion USA (www. accionusa.org) gives $500 credit-builder loans to people with no credit history. While $500 might not sound like much, it could be enough to start a home-based business such as an eBay store.

John and Caprial Pence: How the SBA Guaranteed Loan Program Helped Two Business Owners Get the Financing They Needed

John and Caprial Pence are two of Portland, Oregon's finest cooks and busiest business owners. The two run a growing number of businesses in the Portland area, all focused around fine food. A distinctive aspect of their story is the role that the SBA Guaranteed Loan Program played in their success. The Pences have utilized the SBA loan program twice, and it has been instrumental in helping them build their businesses.

John and Caprial met at the Culinary Institute of America in Hyde Park, New York, where they were both attending school to become chefs. In the mid-1980s, following graduation, they moved to Seattle where they launched their careers. In 1990, Caprial won the James Beard Award for the best chef in the Pacific Northwest. At the same time, she was working on her first cookbook, teaching classes, and appearing on local TV.

In 1992, the Pences decided to move to Portland and bought the old Westmoreland Bistro with private financing. In 1998, they decided to remodel and expand the Bistro when space became available next door. The Pences considered several options for financing. The most realistic alternative, based on the advice of their banker, was an SBA guaranteed loan. The Pences agreed, and the bank facilitated a $260,000 seven-year SBA guaranteed loan. The loan enabled the couple to expand the seating capacity of their restaurant from 26 to 70 tables.

Following the expansion of the restaurant, the Pences decided to diversify and leverage their cooking expertise by opening a cooking school and a cookware shop. A second SBA guaranteed loan, for an identical amount as the first one, made these objectives a reality. The addition of the cooking school and the cookware shop has tripled the Pence's annual revenue.

The future for the Pences and their businesses looks bright. The restaurant initially brought in around $1,000 a day but now brings in $4,000 to $5,000 on an average weekday. The cooking school offers classes and demonstrations nearly every evening, where participants pay from $35 to $135 for hands-on classes or to view special cooking demonstrations. Just recently, the Pences started to bootstrap a television show from the cooking school, and Caprial celebrated the publication of her eighth cookbook.[10]

Equity Funding

Equity funding is obtaining money from an investor. Investors are typically interested in businesses that plan to grow rapidly and can capture fairly large markets. These businesses normally have a unique business idea, a proven management team, and are shooting to capture large markets.

There are two types of equity investors. The first are referred to as *business angels*. Business angels are individuals who invest their personal funds directly into startups. They generally invest between $10,000 and $500,000 in a single company and are looking for companies that have the potential to grow 30–40% per year before they are acquired or go public.[11] Jeffrey Sohl, the director of the University of New Hampshire's Center for Venture Research, estimates that only 10–15% of private companies meet that criterion.[12] The one exception that might help you get your foot in the door with an angel investor, if your business doesn't meet the traditional criteria, is if the purpose of your business is aligned with a personal interest or passion of the investor. For instance, if you're starting a company to make a safer car seat for infant children and meet an angel investor who has an intense interest in child safety products, you could capture the investor's attention even if your firm isn't capable of a 30–40% per year growth rate.

Most business angels remain fairly anonymous and are matched up with business owners through referrals. If you're interested in pursuing angel funding, you should discreetly work your network of acquaintances (bankers, lawyers, accountants, successful entrepreneurs) to see if anyone can make an appropriate introduction.

The second type of equity investor are *venture capitalists*. Venture capital firms are limited partnerships of money managers who raise money in "funds" to invest in startups and growing firms. Some of the better known venture capital firms are Kleiner Perkins, Sequoia Capital, and Redpoint Ventures. Similar to business angels, venture capital firms look for a 30–40% annual return on their investments and a total return over the life of investments of 5 to 20 times the initial investments.[13] The major difference between venture capital firms and business angels is that venture capital firms lend very little money to start-ups (preferring to wait until a firm proves its product and market) and normally don't invest less than $1 million in a single firm. As a result, venture capital funding is only practical for a very small number of business startups.

Grants

A potential source of small business funding that does not get enough attention are *grants*. A grant is a gift of money that does not have to be repaid. While there is no nationwide network for awarding grants to start-up firms, almost every state, city, and local community is trying to find ways to encourage people to start businesses as a means of growing their economies. As a result, there are a growing number of programs available at all levels of government, through the private sector and via foundations, to provide grant money to promising business startups.

Obtaining a grant takes a little detective work. Granting agencies are by nature low-key, so they normally need to be sought out. The best place to inquire about the availability of grants for a particular business is via the SBDC, SCORE, small business incubators, and similar organizations. Although these groups might not have grant money available, they might be able to direct you to organizations that are awarding grants to small businesses in your area.

A typical scenario of a small business that received a grant is provided by Rozalia Williams, the founder of Hidden Curriculum Education (www.hiddencurriculum.com), a for-profit company that offers college life skills courses. To kick-start her business, Williams received a $72,500 grant from Miami Dade Empowerment Trust, a granting agency in Dade County, Florida. The purpose of the Miami Dade Empowerment Trust is to encourage the creation of businesses in disadvantaged neighborhoods of Dade County. The key to William's success, which is true in most grant awarding situations, is that her business fit nicely with the mission of the granting organization, and she was willing to take her business into the areas the granting agency was committed to improving. After being awarded the grant and conducting her college prep courses in four Dade County neighborhoods over a three-year period, Williams received an additional $100,000 loan from the Miami Dade Empowerment Trust to expand her business. There are also private foundations that grant money to both existing and start-up firms. The MacArthur Foundation, for example, is a private grant awarding agency which recently dedicated $2 million to fund projects dealing with digital media and learning.

The federal government has a pair of grant programs for technology firms. The Small Business Innovation Research (SBIR) program is an established program that provides over $1 billion in cash grants per year to small businesses that are working on projects in specific areas. Each year, 10 federal departments and agencies are required by SBIR to reserve a portion of their research and development funds for awards to small businesses. A list of the agencies that participate, along with an explanation of the application process, is available at www.sba.gov/sbir. A privately owned Web site, SBIRworld (www.sbirworld.org), provides useful tips and advice on how to apply for SBIR grants.

The second program, the Small Business Technology Transfer (STTR) program is similar to the SBIR program except it requires the participation of researchers working at universities or other research institutions. Information about the STTR program can be obtained from the Web sites just identified.

Other Potential Sources of Funding

There are other potential sources of funds available for business startups. Similar to locating grants, finding the money takes a little detective work but could be time well spent. For example, there are an increasing number of business plan competitions held across the United States. Many of the competitions offer cash prizes. There are also an increasing number of small business contests sponsored by companies that sell products to small businesses. An example is the Visa Business Breakthrough Contest, which offers five $10,000 awards to businesses that submit essays explaining how they can become more efficient in one of five categories (finance, marketing, organization, team building, and technology). A simple Google search using the keywords "small business contests" will produce similar examples.

More sophisticated ways of obtaining start-up funds involve asking for cash advances from suppliers or potential customers. Some suppliers, if they recognize that your business has the potential to become a regular customer, will invest in your business or provide your business financing to help it get off the ground. Similarly, if you feel that your product or service will add considerable value for a particular customer and save the customer money, the customer might be willing to prepurchase a certain amount of product, which is a way for you to generate start-up funds. If you're buying a franchise, you can typically obtain financing through your franchisor. These alternatives need to be investigated on a case-by-case basis.

There are also ways that business owners tap into personal funds, beyond using savings and cash-on-hand. Examples include borrowing against the cash value of a life insurance policy and tapping into a retirement account. You'll normally need advice from a tax accountant to draw funds from a tax deferred retirement account to finance a business venture.

Summary

It's important to have the right frame of mind regarding money and the start-up process. Often having abundant funds isn't necessarily the best thing. Many business owners look back on their start-up years and recall that it was the lack of money that caused them to get creative and develop sound financial habits—attributes that are still serving them well today. Money is also a topic where it pays to be somewhat of a sleuth. There are many sources of start-up funds available, such as grants, business plan competitions, and SBDC guaranteed loans. These sources of funds, however, have to be sought out and tracked down to make an impact on a new company.

The next chapter focuses on the myth that it takes a lot of business experience to start a successful firm. Because most of the businesses we deal with are established companies, it's easy to believe that they were started by experienced business people and have always run as smoothly as they do. In reality, most businesses were started by people just like you. There are also many forms of experience that are helpful in the business start-up process. You might have vastly underestimated the value of the skills and experiences that you presently have.

Endnotes

1   "How Much Money Does It Take to Start a Small Business?" *Wells Fargo/Gallup Small Business Index*, (San Francisco: Wells Fargo Bank), August 15, 2006.

2   "Inc. 500," *Inc.*, Special Issue, 2006.

3   Jessica Livingston, *Founders at Work: Stories of Startups' Early Days* (New York: Apress, 2008), 259.

4   Jack Canfield and Mark Victor Hansen, *Chicken Soup for the Entrepreneur's Soul* (Deerfield Beach: Health Communications, Inc., 2006), 47.

5   Livingston, *Founders at Work*, 444.

6   Jay Ebben and Alec Johnson, "Bootstrapping in Small Firms: An Empirical Analysis of Change Over Time," *Journal of Business Venturing* 21 (2006): 851–865.

7   Ladies Who Launch, accessed September 12, 2007 (see chap. 1, n. 4).

8   Ladies Who Launch, accessed April 7, 2007 (see chap. 1, n. 4).

9   Ibid.

10 Caprial and John's Kitchen home page, http://www.caprialandjohnskitchen.com (accessed September 14, 2007); Shelly Herochik, "Restaurateurs Fit More on the Plate With Help of Loan Program," *Bizjournal*, http://www.bizjournals.com (accessed September 14, 2007).

11 Jim Melloan, "Angels With Angels," *Inc.*, July 2005.

12 Ibid.

13 PricewaterhouseCoopers, *Three Keys to Obtaining Venture Capital* (New York: PricewaterhouseCoopers, 2001).

CHAPTER 4

Myth No. 4:
It Takes a Great Deal of Business Experience to Start a Successful Business

Truth No. 4:
Successful Businesses Are Started by People with All Levels of Business Experience

Introduction

One of the most pervasive myths that inhibit people from starting their own businesses is the notion that it takes a great deal of business experience to start a successful business. It's easy to understand where this notion comes from. Most of the businesses we deal with are established companies with employees, customers, well-established processes, and track records of success. Because we didn't see these businesses when they were young, it's easy to believe that they've always run as smoothly as they do today. In addition, most of the business founders we know about, such as Bill Gates (Microsoft) and Michael Dell (Dell), seem to have done everything right in building their businesses. If someone told you that each of these individuals had substantial business experience before they started their companies, there would be no reason to disbelieve them.

The problem with these depictions is that they create misconceptions about the way businesses start and evolve and the amount of expertise it takes to start them. Most businesses start small and grow over time—it's just that we rarely see them when they're first getting started. Wal-Mart, for example, started with a single store in Bentonville, Arkansas. And there are many examples of firms, including Microsoft and Dell, which were started by people with no business experience at all. In fact, most of the businesses we profile in this book were started by people with little or no prior business experience. Examples include darynkagen.com (started by a former CNN reporter), Dynamic Interventions (started by three school psychologists), Flavorx (started by a man working in his parents' pharmacy), and The Pampered Chef (started by a homemaker).

There are businesses that do take a substantial amount of experience to successfully start and run. Most financial services and medical product companies, for example, are started by people with deep industry backgrounds and business expertise.

There are also technical aspects of starting a business such as finance and accounting, which take time and effort to learn and perfect, regardless of the type of business. In these instances, people who have business experience have a leg-up on those who don't. It's also easy to envision the advantage that someone who has managed people and run a successful business before might have over someone who hasn't.

Still, there are many examples of people who have started successful businesses without prior business experience. In the absence of knowing their individual stories, however, it's easy to believe the myth. Regrettably, this misconception causes capable people to never seriously investigate starting their own businesses. Without having information to the contrary, however, it's easy for people to assume that their lack of business experience is too difficult an obstacle to overcome.

To further dispel the myth that it takes a great deal of business experience to start a successful business and to provide suggestions to people who remain uneasy about their lack of business experience, this chapter is divided into three sections. The first section provides insight into the role that prior business experience plays in the business start-up process. The second section focuses on business opportunities that minimize the need for substantial business experience. The third section focuses on techniques that help people overcome the lack of prior business experience as they launch their own businesses.

Insights Into the Role That Prior Business Experience Plays in the Business Start-Up Process

In most start-up situations, there are two benefits to having prior business experience. The first is the acquisition of specific skills. If you are proficient at accounting or know the ins and outs of hiring and managing people, those skills are helpful in starting and growing a business. The second benefit is a simple assimilation of how businesses run and what makes them successful. Simply by being part of the business world, people gain a sense of what works and what doesn't work in particular business situations.

The question then becomes how valuable is prior business experience in a start-up setting and how much of an obstacle is not having this experience. Would Dell, darynkagen.com, and the other companies we've highlighted that were started by people with no business experience be stronger today if they had been started by experienced businesspeople? In addition, are there forms of business experience that might be a detriment rather than an advantage in a start-up setting? And how much does practical experience count? If I've worked as an auto mechanic all my life and would like to open a store that sells customized auto accessories, am I capable of starting that business, or do I need to get some business experience first?

The sections that follow provide three insights about the role of prior business experience in the start-up process. As you read through each, give careful thought to how the insight affects your own views on the topic. Many people overcome the fear that a lack of business experience is too large an obstacle by becoming more familiar with the start-up process and by gaining a better appreciation of the value of the other skills and capabilities they possess.

Nearly Everyone Feels Inadequate on Some Level

The first insight regarding the role of prior business experience in the start-up process is to keep the role of business experience in perspective. It's only one type of experience. There are many forms of experience that potentially affect the success of a new business, including business experience, practical experience in the specific area the business will operate in, sales experience, and leadership experience. Virtually no one has an ideal set of experiences as a foundation for starting a new business. Because of this, nearly everyone feels inadequate on some level. While the auto mechanic who wants to open a store to sell customized auto parts might feel inadequate because he doesn't have business experience, a seasoned business person with the same idea could feel inadequate because he doesn't know as much about repairing or modifying cars.

Feelings of inadequacy are also prompted by the sheer number of tasks people realize they'll be responsible for if they start their own businesses. This facet of business ownership causes people with business backgrounds to question whether their range of experience is adequate. For example, you might be a graphic artist who wants to open your own shop and have experience managing a staff and overseeing a budget, but might still feel uneasy because you have no experience in marketing or sales.

The overarching point of these observations is that nearly everyone feels inadequate in some aspect of starting a business. This emotion is so strong that some business owners say that their innermost fear is that their customers or employees will discover how much they really "don't know" about the business they've started. The first step to overcoming fear of inadequacy is to give yourself credit for the experiences you've had. If you think about the jobs you've had, the volunteer work you've done, the work you did in school, your family experiences, and so forth, your breadth of experience is probably more expansive than you first imagined. The second step is to boost your own self-efficacy for starting a business. Self-efficacy refers to your belief that you can perform a specific task (like starting a business). Several steps for boosting your self-efficacy for starting a business were discussed in Chapter 1, including reading books and articles about ordinary people who started successful businesses and participating in small business workshops and events where you get encouragement from business owners.

Certain Types of Business Experience Might Actually Hurt Rather Than Help You

The second insight is that there are certain types of business experiences that might actually hurt rather than help in your efforts to start a business. This heads-up refers to the difficulties some people have transitioning from a corporate environment to a small business, so these circumstances might not apply to you. Still, for those fitting this profile, it is important information to have.

The primary complication that occurs when people from corporate backgrounds try to start their own businesses is they have trouble adjusting to the constraints inherent to the start-up setting. It's easy to envision the frustrations that someone might experience coming from a resource-rich large firm to trying to launch a business on a razor-thin budget. In addition, the skills that a person develops in a corporate setting are often not a good fit for a small firm. This point is made by Guy Kawasaki, a well-known investor and entrepreneur:

> *"Success in a big organization doesn't guarantee success in a startup. The skills needed in each context are different. A vice president of Microsoft (with its established brand, infinite resources, and 100 percent market share) may not be the right person for a 'two guys in a garage operation.'"*[1]

This mismatch of skills can also extend to management techniques and business processes. A person who has worked for IBM, Hewlett-Packard, and Motorola might have an impressive resume, but there is no guarantee that the IBM, Hewlett-Packard, or Motorola ways of doing things is appropriate for a specific small business. One silver lining to having limited or no business experience is that you're able to approach the challenge of starting a business with fresh eyes and no preconceptions. In some instances, simple commonsense management, applied by someone with limited or no business experience, might be more effective than the more sophisticated techniques that would be applied by someone with more business experience.

Domain-Specific Experience Is Often as Important as Business Experience

The third insight regarding the role of business experience in the start-up process is that *domain-specific experience* is often as important as business experience. Domain-specific experience is experience in the specific area in which your start-up will compete.

There are many companies that are started by people with unique insights into specific areas as a result of their jobs, hobbies, family responsibilities, or intense interest in particular areas. These people may or may not have business experience, but it's their domain-specific experience that is the motivating factor for starting the business.

An example of a business that was launched and is now being successfully run largely as a result of domain-specific experience is provided by Tish Ciravolo, the founder of Daisy Rock Guitars, a company that makes guitars just for women. Daisy Rock guitars are stylish, have feminine names (e.g., Atomic Pink, Power Pink, and Rainbow Sparkle), and incorporate design features that accommodate a woman's smaller hands and build. Ciravolo started playing the guitar when she was in high school and has devoted a large portion of her life to playing in bands and helping girls and women become acquainted with the guitar. The motivation for Daisy Rock grew from Ciravolo's desire to provide her own daughters and other females with something she didn't have when she was growing up—a guitar designed specifically for women. Commenting on this desire, Ciravolo said:

> *"When the time comes, I want their experience [referring to her daughters Nicole and Sophia] as musicians to be different from when I was growing up, when every guitar available was designed with men in mind. I want them to be able to walk into a music store anywhere and be able to find something made with them in mind. Daisy Rock is not about making me rich and famous or being a hero to anyone. It's simply an opportunity to leave a legacy for my kids and provide females with great instruments designed with them in mind."[2]*

This exemplifies how domain-specific knowledge, like Ciravolo's familiarity with the difficulties women face in playing guitars designed for men, provides insights that can lead to business ideas and actual products. No amount of business experience would have provided Ciravolo the insight she gleaned about guitars through her actual experiences. Founded in 2000, Daisy Rock's annual sales are now in excess of $2 million.

There are many other examples, some of which have been highlighted in this book, of people who have drawn upon domain-specific experience to get their businesses off the ground. An example is Doug and Lisa Powell, the business owners introduced in Chapter 2 who started Type 1 and Type 2 Tools, the company that provides age-appropriate motivational and educational material for child diabetics. It was Doug and Lisa Powell's familiarity with their daughter's disease and their skills as graphic designers that provided them the insights and capabilities needed to start the company.

Obtaining Domain-Specific Experience Over Time

One thing people thinking about starting their own businesses should consider, particularly if they are uneasy about the amount of business experience they have, is to start their businesses part-time and accumulate experience as they go. While this approach isn't possible in all situations, it can apply in more circumstances than you might think. By starting a business part-time, you can gain valuable experience, tuck away the money you earn, and find out if you really like the business before you quit your current job.

What's needed to start a business part-time is a little creativity regarding how to do it and a commitment to learn as much as possible along the way. For example, if your dream is to open a barbeque restaurant, you could start by catering barbeque on weekends as a way of learning the business and experimenting with recipes. If you'd like to open your own Web site design business, you could start

> on a freelance basis and obtain jobs through venues
> such as Elance (www.elance.com) and Craigslist
> (www.craigslist.com). If you make crafts and envision
> opening a craft store someday, you could start by selling
> your products at craft shows and through local stores on
> a consignment basis. That way you'll learn what sells and
> what doesn't sell and get a sense of whether you really
> want to operate a craft store full-time.

Opportunities That Minimize the Need for Substantial Business Experience

One approach that people utilize to compensate for a lack of business experience is to pursue a business opportunity that minimizes the need for business experience. Many businesses require their founders to basically develop the businesses from scratch. In these instances, if the founders do not have prior business experience, they have to quickly get up-to-speed and learn the basics of starting a business. While business owners are often able to accomplish these objectives, there is an alternative. The alternative is to pursue a business opportunity in which the fundamentals of the business have already been thought out, and the business owner's responsibility is to run the business. Some approaches that fit this profile are franchising, direct sales, and businesses that have well-established business models.

Franchising

Franchising is a form of business ownership in which a firm that already has a successful product or service (franchisor) licenses its trademark and method of doing business to other businesses (franchisees) in exchange for an initial franchise fee and an ongoing royalty. The cost of buying into a franchise system varies, as shown in Table 4.1. The total initial investment includes the franchise fee, the costs associated with getting the franchise up and running (which vary by franchise), and any other fees that are part of the franchise agreement. The ongoing royalty fee, which is usually around 6%, is based on a percentage of weekly or monthly gross income.

Table 4.1 Initial Cost to the Franchisee of Opening a Franchise

Franchise Organization	One-Time Franchise Fee	Ongoing Royalty	Total Initial Investment
Subway	$15,000	8%	$74,900 to $222,800
Curves	$24,900 to $39,900	5% to 6%	$31,400 to $53,500
Great Clips	$25,000	6%	$98,900 to $184,700
CruiseOne Inc.	$9,800	3%	$9,800 to $25,400
WIN Home Inspection	$25,000	7%	$45,600 to $57,600
1-800-GOT-JUNK?	$20,000+	8%	$73,500 to $98,900
Cold Stone Creamery	$42,000	6%	$294,300 to $438,900

There are two primary advantages to buying a franchise as opposed to opening a business of your own. First, franchising provides a small business owner the opportunity to own a business using a tested and refined business system. This attribute reduces the amount of prior business experience needed to participate in most franchises. In addition, the trademark that comes with the franchise proves instant legitimacy for the business. For instance, if you're interested in opening a fitness center for women, you'll likely attract more customers by opening a Curves or Contours Express franchise than a new, independently owned business. The second advantage to buying a franchise is that the franchisor typically provides training, technical expertise, and other forms of ongoing support. For example, if you buy into a Contours Express franchise, your initial investment gets you Contours Express's exclusive 16-piece line of fitness equipment, cue tapes, wall charts, training on all business systems, and the support of a fitness professional who will help you open your center and run it for the first few days. Moving forward, you have access to a quarterly marketing package, an annual convention, and periodic training seminars. This type of training and support is what attracts people that lack business experience to the franchise option. According to Daren Carter, Contours Express's founder, 99% of the company's franchisees had no formal fitness training before they purchased a Contours Express franchise.[3] This level of inexperience is typical for a franchise system. In fact, some systems shy away from people with prior experience in the field the franchise operates in, fearing that they could have too many preconceived notions about how to run the business.

The main disadvantages of buying a franchise are the costs involved and the loss of some of your independence as a business owner. As shown in Table 4.1, there are substantial costs involved with buying into most franchise systems, and the royalties are permanent. While there are costs associated with opening an independent business, you get to keep 100% of your profits. In regard to independence, many franchise systems are sticklers about doing things in a very specific manner. McDonald's and other fast-food franchises, for example, are very strict in terms of their restaurants' appearance and how their food is prepared. As a result, franchising is typically not a good fit for people who like to experiment with their own ideas and are independently minded.

Ultimately, franchising represents an attractive middle ground for many people. So says John Cummings, the purchaser of a PostNet franchise. A PostNet franchise is similar to a FedEx Kinko's store. After a 21-year career with Bristol-Myers, Cummings took a buyout and spent a year deciding on what to do next. Commenting on why he settled on a PostNet franchise rather than opening his own business, Cummings said:

> *"I wanted to get what I call the best of both worlds—the support of a proven system in an environment that's really entrepreneurial. I felt a franchise was the best way to do that."*[4]

One note of caution—you should be careful if you decide to buy into a franchise system. While there are many excellent franchise systems to choose from, some systems never live up to the level of support promised. The best way to check out the merits of a franchisor is to ask for the names, addresses, and phone numbers of several of the franchisor's current franchisees and then call these individuals and ask them about their experiences. You can also ask for a copy of the franchisor's Uniform Franchise Offering Circular (UFOC), which is a document that contains 23 categories of information about the background and financial health of the franchisor. Section 20 of the document contains contact information for all of the system's current franchisees.

Direct Sales

The second type of business opportunity that minimizes the amount of prior business experience that's needed is *direct sales*. While most people cringe when they hear the words "direct sales" (or multi-level marketing), there are legitimate direct sales opportunities. Currently, there are over 14 million people in the United States involved in direct sales (full-time and part-time), and the industry generates roughly $30.5 billion in annual sales.[5] Well-known companies in the industry include Tupperware, The Pampered Chef, Avon, Mary Kay, World Book, and Discovery Toys.

Many people have negative feelings toward the direct sales industry because they have either personally been subjected to a high pressure sales pitch or know someone who has. Although the industry as a whole suffers as a result of these types of sales tactics, not all direct sales firms fit this stereotype, and there is an increasing number of highly legitimate opportunities. An example of a direct sales organization that exemplifies the good in the industry is The Pampered Chef, discussed in Chapter 2. The integrity and stature of the company is such that it was acquired by Berkshire Hathaway in 2002. Berkshire Hathaway is controlled by Warren Buffett, one of the most respected and well-known investors in the world. In the foreword to the book, *The Pampered Chef*, in which Christopher chronicles the history of the company, Buffett writes:

> *"The Pampered Chef is truly loved by its customers because it has found a need and filled it exceptionally well, helping everyday home cooks to become masters of their own home kitchens and making mealtime preparation quick, easy, and fun. It also offers its consultants an incomparable business opportunity, allowing men and women to build a home-based business of their own, based on Doris Christopher's personal blueprint for success. When you read the profiles of The Pampered Chef's Kitchen Consultants in Chapter 8, you may wonder what you're doing in your nine-to-five cubicle while these folks are happy cooking their way to fame and fortune."[6]*

Most people start with an organization like The Pampered Chef part-time and only make it a full-time job if they do extremely well. The sales typically take place through in-home sales demonstrations or parties, although an increasing percentage of direct sales is taking place online. In addition to selling the product, you'll also recruit others to sell the product for you. You then receive a percentage of your recruits' sales, just like the person that recruited you receives a percentage of your sales. One of the lures of direct sales is that you can usually get started for a few hundred dollars, which gets you your initial inventory and sales material. Most direct sales organizations provide you with training, marketing material, and ongoing support. You also get a mentor and champion in the person that recruited you. The person that recruited you has a vested interest in your success, since he or she receives a commission on your sales.

If you go the direct sales route, make sure you associate with a reputable organization. One way to minimize the chances that you'll select a company you will later regret is to restrict your selection to organizations that are members of the Direct Selling Association (www.dsa.org), a highly respected industry trade group. To become a member of the Direct Selling Association, a firm has to go through a rigorous one-year application process and abide by the organization's Code of Ethics. Only 216 of more than 1,000 direct sales organizations that exist are currently members. If an organization is not a member of the Direct Sales Association, and you are still interested in joining, you should, at a minimum, check the company's history with your local Better Business Bureau, your state's Attorney General, and the Federal Trade Commission.

Azante Jewelry: How One Direct Sales System Got Started

Azante Jewelry was started by Cheri Larson in 2003. The original idea for the business was to sell jewelry through boutiques in Door County, Wisconsin. Shortly before the business was launched, a friend asked Larson if she'd be willing to show her jewelry to a group of her friends. Larson agreed, and that gathering turned into $1,400 in sales. It also got Larson thinking that maybe a direct sales model was better than selling her jewelry through boutiques.

After a few similar outings, Larson decided to commit to the direct sales approach and spent the next year and a half researching the direct sales industry and the competition in her area. She also attended several small business seminars hosted by the Urban Hope Entrepreneurial Center in Green Bay, Wisconsin. The seminars focused on topics such as writing a business plan, researching markets, and understanding financial issues.

Larson formally rolled out her business in 2003 with two sales consultants. Her role was to design and oversee the manufacturing of the jewelry and encourage and motivate her independent sales force. Today, Larson employs five people at her Green Bay office and has 75 independent sales consultants. The thing that differentiates Azante Jewelry from jewelry that can be bought in stores is its quality and workmanship. Each piece is hand crafted and consists of a unique design.

Larson has no desire to grow Azante Jewelry quickly. Although she'd like to reach the heights of The Pampered Chef someday, that goal won't come soon. Still, Larson has high hopes for both the size of the business and her ability to grow her ranks of independent sales consultants. Commenting on the holistic nature of her business, Larson said:

"There's an opportunity to get quite large. The important thing is to offer an employment opportunity to women who might be stay-at-home moms or just want to work part-time."[7]

Businesses That Have Well-Established Business Models

The third type of business opportunity that minimizes the amount of prior business experience that's needed is starting a business that has a well-established business model. A firm's business model describes how it operates and makes money. There are a number of businesses that have a fairly standard business model. Following these models negates, in part, the prior business experience needed to launch and run one of these businesses.

An example of a business with a well-established business model is a bed & breakfast. There are literally dozens of books available that provide advice about how to open and run a successful bed & breakfast. These books are very hands-on and contain worksheets and formulas that help estimate the cost of opening a bed & breakfast and provide instruction for how to manage day-to-day operations. To illustrate the strength and diversity of books that are available, a sample is provided in Table 4.2. There are also workshops held periodically across the country about how to open and operate a successful bed & breakfast. Several trade associations support the industry. An example is the Professional Association of Innkeepers (www.paii.org), which was founded in 1988 and now has over 3,000 members.[8] There are also bed & breakfast organizations that service smaller areas. Examples include the Wisconsin Bed and Breakfast Association (www.wbba.com) and Inn Virginia, the Bed & Breakfast Association of Virginia (http://innvirginia.org). Both organizations offer seminars for people thinking about opening their own bed & breakfast. A similar assortment of books, workshops, seminars, and trade associations is available for other businesses.

Table 4.2   Books That Provide Instruction for How to Open a Bed & Breakfast

Title and Author	Publisher and Year Published
How to Open a Financially Successful Bed & Breakfast or Small Hotel by Laura Arduser and Douglas R. Brown	Atlantic Publishing Company (2004)
Complete Idiot's Guide to Running a Bed and Breakfast by Susannah Craig and Park Davis	Alpha (2001)
How to Open and Operate a Bed & Breakfast (8th Edition) by Jan Stankus	Globe Pequot (2007)
How to Start and Operate Your Own Bed-and-Breakfast: Down-To-Earth Advice from an Award-Winning B&B Owner by Martha W. Murphy and Amelia R. Seton	Owl Books (1994)
So—You Want to Be an Innkeeper by Jo Ann M. Bell, Susan Brown, Mary Davis, and Pat Hardy	Chronicle Books (2004)

Another example of a business that someone with minimal prior business experience could open is an eBay store because there is an established method for opening one. eBay has a physical location on the eBay Web site (www.ebay.com) that a person can utilize to list the things he or she has for sale and to interact with customers. While you don't need an eBay store to sell items on eBay, most serious eBay sellers have one. eBay makes it extremely easy to set up a store. An easy-to-follow set of instructions is available on the eBay Web site, and the company offers a complementary selling consultation to anyone in the form of a one-on-one phone conversation with an eBay consultant. In addition, eBay makes forums available for eBay sellers to ask questions and discuss ideas with one another, and eBay University (www.ebayuniversity.com) provides access to training material and lists the itinerary for eBay seminars that are held in over 30 cities each year. There are also a large number of books that have been written by independent authors that provide instructions and tips for how to open an eBay store. The net result is that there are now reportedly over one million people worldwide making their living selling merchandise on eBay.

The overall point of this discussion isn't to draw attention to bed & breakfast businesses and eBay stores. The larger message is that there are many business opportunities, aside from franchising and direct sales, where the nuts-and-bolts of the business have been carefully thought out and are documented in easily accessible forms. This set of factors lessens the need for prior business experience in launching and running these businesses.

Techniques That Help People Overcome the Lack of Business Experience

Another approach that people take to compensate for a lack of business experience is to partner with someone who has business experience or join a support group. In fact, one of the most common reasons business partnerships form is that the individuals involved realize that they don't have sufficient experience and skill to launch businesses on their own. In addition, there are a growing number of social networks and forums that business owners can join to get support and advice from more experienced business people.

The two techniques covered in this section that help people overcome their lack of business experience are forming business partnerships and joining support groups/participating in online forums.

Forming Partnerships

An important decision a business owner faces is whether to start a business alone or whether to include a partner. A total of 56% of the firms included in the 2007 *Inc.* 5,000, which is the 5,000 fastest-growing private companies in the United States, were started by two or more people.[9] In general, it's believed that new ventures started by two or more people have an advantage over those started by an individual, because a team brings more talent, resources, ideas, and professional contacts to a new venture than does a sole business owner. In addition, the emotional and psychological support that the partners in a new business can offer one another can be an important element in a firm's success.

The ideal partnership brings together people with complementary experiences and skills. For example, an individual with technical skills, like a computer programmer, might want to seek out a partner who has business experience to create a more well-rounded team. This scenario played out for Kabir Shahani and Chris Hahn, the cofounders of Appature, a software company that targets the healthcare industry. In this instance, Hahn sought out Shahani to create a partnership in which their respective skills complement each other's. Shahani recalls:

> "He [Hahn] had a lot of faith in my skills, and I feel really fortunate that he did. I'll never forget that conversation. We were sitting in a Thai restaurant in the International district [of Seattle], and he said, 'Look, I can build anything, and I think you can sell anything, so let's do it.'"[10]

The biggest mistake people make in forming partnerships is partnering with others who have the same skills and same deficiencies that they have. The reason this happens is that people tend to draw from their circles of acquaintances when selecting a partner. Engineers know other engineers, physical therapists know other physical therapists, cooks know other cooks, and so forth. Try to resist the temptation of partnering with one of your peers. The best partnerships are the ones that bring together people with complementary skills.

You should be careful when selecting a partner because starting a business with another person is a major undertaking and places a strain on the best of relationships. This is why picking a business partner is often compared to selecting a spouse—it's a long-term relationship that is painful to terminate. One necessity in forming a business partnership is to create a written partnership agreement. You can get help doing this through your local Small Business Development Center, SCORE chapter, or an attorney.

There is also a full complement of small business legal forms, including a standard partnership agreement, available at www.findlaw.com. If you don't have a formal partnership agreement, you leave yourself open to the possibilities of serious disagreements down the road.

Joining Support Groups and Participating in Online Forums

Another technique business owners use to compensate for a lack of business experience is to join support groups and participate in online forums. All business owners need periodic advice and support. In addition, the simple act of hanging out with other business owners, whether in person or online, can be extremely helpful. A theme repeated throughout this book is that knowing the stories of other business owners can boost your own self-efficacy or belief that you can start and run a successful business. Joining a support group and/or regularly participating in online forums are ways of guaranteeing yourself that you will regularly interact with other business owners.

There is an increasing number of support groups available for business owners. Most of them target a specific demographic or focus on a particular industry. For example, there are several support groups for women business owners. An example is the National Association for Women Business Owners (www.nawbo.org), which provides services on a national level and supports 90 local chapters across the United States. The local chapters sponsor dinner meetings, lunch meetings, and other events where women business owners listen to speakers, participate in business-related workshops, and network with one another. Most of the local chapters host their own Web sites to highlight their events. An example is the Web site of the Orlando Chapter of the National Association for Women Business Owners, which is available at www.nawboorlando.org.

If you're looking for a support group in your area and can't find one, check the Meetup Web site. Meetup (www.meetup.com) is an online platform that allows individuals to organize local groups via the Web. Once a group is formed, its members "meet up" on a regular basis offline. The service, which was launched in 2002, has struck a chord, and there are currently over 13,000 Meetup groups worldwide, which focus on topics as diverse as cooking and flying kites. A growing number of these groups focus on some aspect of small business or entrepreneurship. To find out if there is a small business Meetup group in your area, simply type "small business" in the search box on the Meetup front page and enter your zip code. A sample of small business Meetup groups that were meeting when this chapter was written is included below. If there isn't a Meetup group in your area, you can start one.

- The Metro Detroit Small Business Meetup Group
- The Cincinnati Small Business Help Group
- Arizona & Easy Valley eBay Seller's Meetup Group
- Small Business Strategies for Success (Stone Mountain, GA)
- The San Diego E-Business Owner's Meetup Group
- The Overland Park (Kansas) Work At Home Meetup Group

There are also a growing number of online forums that have been developed to provide small business owners support and advice. An example is StartupNation (www.startupnation.com).

The StartupNation Web site sponsors online forums for small business owners that cover topics such as selecting a business for yourself, business planning, developing your invention, and accounting and financial management. It also features open-ended forums such as "coffee talk," where small business owners can chat with one another about any topic that is on their minds. The general tone of the forums tends to be supportive and upbeat, which is exactly what many small business owners need. A small business forum that is more specific is the Small Business Computing and E-Commerce Forum (www.smallbusinesscomputing.com). This forum is similar to the one just described but focuses strictly on technology issues.

Summary

In the vast majority of cases, a lack of business experience isn't a reason to stop someone from starting a business. No one starts a business with the ideal set of experiences and skills. The collection of experiences and skills that you presently have, along with a willingness to choose the business you start carefully and learn as you go, will serve you well if you decide to start a business of your own.

The next chapter focuses on the myth that the best business ideas are already taken. By looking around, it's easy to see why this myth is so prevalent—there are literally thousands of products to choose from. But in reality, people come up with new business ideas everyday—many of which make a real difference in people's lives. In Chapter 5, we show you how to identify and generate new business ideas.

Endnotes

1   Guy Kawasaki, *The Art of the Start* (New York: Portfolio, 2004), 102.

2   Daisy Rock home page, http://www.daisyrock.com (accessed September 20, 2007).

3   Franchise Gator home page, http://www.franchisegator.com (accessed September 20, 2007).

4   CJ Prince, "Buying Balance by Finding a Franchise," *Success Magazine*, http://www.successmagazine.com/article.php?article_id=195 (accessed September 20, 2007).

5   Direct Sales Association home page, http://www.dsa.org (accessed September 21, 2007).

6   Doris Christopher, *The Pampered Chef* (New York: Doubleday, 2005), ix.

7   Leah Call, "Direct Sales Success," *Wisconsin Entrepreneur's Network*, http://www.wenportal.org (accessed September 20, 2007).

8   Professional Association of Innkeepers home page, http://www.paii.org (accessed September 21, 2007).

9   *Inc.*, November 20, 2007.

10   nPost, accessed September 22, 2007 (see chap. 1, n. 11).

Myth No. 5:
The Best Business Ideas Are Already Taken

Truth No. 5:
There Are an Infinite Number of Possibilities for Good Business Ideas

Introduction

O f all the myths surrounding business ownership, the notion that the best business ideas are already taken is the most exaggerated. It simply isn't true. New businesses based on new ideas are started everyday. In addition, there is nothing wrong with starting a business that's a slight variation of something that already exists. In fact, most new businesses do not launch revolutionary new products or services—they are just too expensive to bring to market. Though there are exceptions. FedEx, for example, was started in the 1970s on the revolutionary idea of creating a system to facilitate the overnight delivery of packages. Far more common are businesses such as The Pampered Chef, which sells unique but not revolutionary kitchen products, and Daisy Rock, which sells guitars that are designed specifically for women but are otherwise regular guitars.

The reason it's easy to believe the myth that the best business ideas are already taken is that it seems as if the marketplace as crowded and full of products that meet every conceivable need. In many instances, this perception is correct. Think of how many different choices we all have for car insurance, credit cards, house paint, and tires. These are products in mature industries where it is difficult to think of new business ideas. But for someone who's thinking about starting a business, there are ample opportunities elsewhere. For example, think about how society is changing. The aging of the population alone is spawning new business ideas almost daily—from fitness centers designed specifically for older people to cell phones that have large buttons and bright screens to make them easier for older people to use and see. There are also many problems that remain unsolved. This sentiment is captured by Philip Kotler, a marketing expert, who said:

> *"Think about problems. People complain about it being hard to sleep through the night, get rid of clutter in their homes, find an affordable vacation, trace their family origins, get rid of garden weeds, and so on. As the late John Gardner, founder of Common Cause, observed: 'Every problem is a brilliantly disguised opportunity.'"*[1]

The gist of Kotler's point is that potential business owners have fertile ground in which to discern new business ideas. If you agree with this sentiment, it makes more sense to believe that the best business ideas have yet to be discovered rather than the best business ideas are already taken.

How, then, are new business ideas discovered? And what are the attributes of effective versus ineffective ideas? Even if we've convinced you by now that the best business ideas aren't already taken, you're still left with the task of coming up with a business idea as the foundation for starting your own business. To address these issues and further dispel the myth that the best business ideas are already taken, this chapter is divided into two sections. The first section focuses on the three most common sources of new business ideas. The second section focuses on techniques that potential business owners use to explore these sources and generate business ideas.

Three Most Common Sources of New Business Ideas

The first step in discerning new business ideas is to understand where business ideas come from. In our experience, business ideas emerge from three sources: changing environmental trends, unsolved problems, and gaps in the marketplace. A recognition and understanding of these sources is helpful to people who are trying to identify business ideas for themselves. Once you understand the importance of each of these sources, you'll be much more likely to look for opportunities and ideas that fit each profile. One thing to be careful about as you read through each source is immediately thinking of an idea and quickly moving forward with it. Business owners often think of many ideas before they settle on the idea that becomes their business—so don't rush the process. It's also important not to select an idea simply because it is appealing. Although the conviction and passion for an idea is vitally important, the key to the selection process is to identify a product or service that people need and are willing to buy, not one that seems fun or attractive to sell.

Now let's look at the three most common sources of business ideas, as reflected in Figure 5.1.

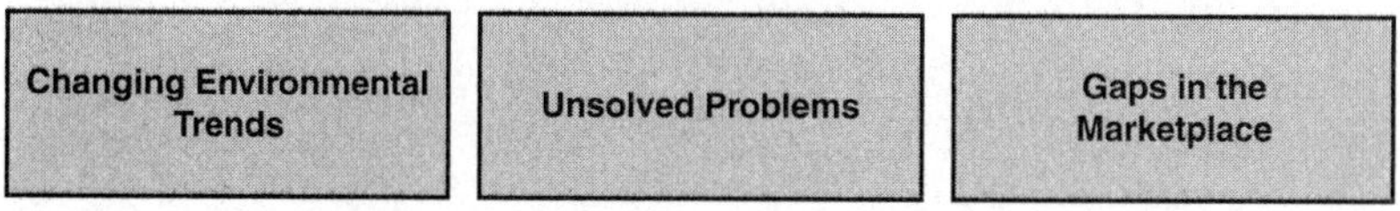

Changing Environmental Trends	Unsolved Problems	Gaps in the Marketplace

Figure 5.1 *Three sources of new business ideas*

A Critical Issue When Searching for a Business Idea: Selecting an Idea That Can be Sold Into a Niche Market

One rule-of-thumb that you should adhere to when searching for a business idea is to select an idea that can be sold into a niche market.

A *niche market* is a place within a larger market segment that represents a narrower group of customers with similar needs. Starting by selling to a niche market allows a firm to focus on serving a specialized market very well instead of trying to be everything to everyone in a broad market, which is nearly impossible for a new firm. The challenge in identifying an attractive niche market is to find a market that's large enough for the proposed business but is yet small enough to avoid attracting larger competitors, at least during the time it takes for the new business to successfully get off the ground. An example of a company that has selected a niche market that meets these criteria is Dogster (www.dogster.com), a social networking site for dog owners. The site allows its users to create profiles for their dogs, participate in dog-related forums, post photos and video clips of their dogs, and perform a number of other activities. The site, which was started from scratch in 2004 with its sister site, Catster (www.catster.com), now has over 275,000 human members, 340,000 photos of dogs and cats, and a collection of blue-chip advertisers, including Disney and Target. Although the firm operates in the $36 billion pet industry, it has carved out a specialized niche market for itself and is reported to be operating in the black and generating more than a million dollars a year in advertising revenue.

As Dogster gains momentum and financial resources, it may grow beyond this specialized market but has gotten off to a good start largely because it has remained laser-focused on a clearly defined niche market (social networking for dog and cat owners) rather than spreading itself too thin in the larger pet industry.

Changing Environmental Trends

The first source of new business ideas is changing environmental trends. The most important trends for people to follow in thinking of starting their own business are economic trends, social trends, technological advances, and political action and regulatory changes. Changes in these areas often provide the impetus for new business ideas. When looking at environmental trends to discern new business ideas, there are two caveats to keep in mind. First, it's important to distinguish between trends and fads. New businesses typically do not have the resources to ramp up quickly enough to take advantage of a fad. Second, even though we discuss each trend individually, they are interconnected and should be considered simultaneously when brainstorming new business ideas. For example, one reason the Apple iPod is so popular is because it benefits from several trends converging at the same time, including teenagers and young adults with increased disposable income (economic trend), an increasingly mobile population (social trend), and the continual miniaturization of electronics (technological trend). If any of these trends weren't present, the iPod wouldn't be as successful as it is.

Table 5.1 provides examples of how changes in environmental trends have provided the impetus for new business ideas and new businesses. The following is a discussion of each trend and how changes in a trend provide openings for new business and product ideas.

Table 5.1   Companies Started to Take Advantage of Changes in Environmental Trends

Changing Environmental Trend	Resulting New Business Opportunities	Companies That Resulted
Economic Trends		
Search for alternatives to traditional fossil fuels like gasoline and diesel fuel	Ethanol, biodiesel, solar power, wind-generated power	SolFocus, Seattle Biodiesel, Misole
Teenagers with more cash and disposable income	Designer clothes, compact discs, MP3 players, game consoles	Hot Topic, Karma Loop, SanDisk

continues

Table 5.1   Continued

Changing Environmental Trend	Resulting New Business Opportunities	Companies That Resulted
Social Trends		
Increased interest in different, tastier, and healthier food	Healthy-fare restaurants, organic foods, healthy-focused grocery stores	Chipotle, White Wave, Whole Foods
Increased interest in fitness as the results of new medical information warns of the hazards of being overweight	Fitness centers, in-house exercise equipment, health food stores	Curves, Espresso Fitness, GNC Nutrition Center
Technological Advances		
Development of the Internet	E-commerce, improved supply chain management, improved communication, social networking	Google, Amazon.com, Travelocity, MySpace.com
Miniaturization of electronics	Laptop computers, MP3 players, PDAs	Digital Lifestyle Outfitters, Palm, Research In Motion
Political and Regulatory Changes		
Increased EPA and OSHA standards	Consulting companies, software to monitor compliance	ESS, PrimaTech, Compliance Consulting Services, Inc.
Sarbanes Oxley Act of 2002	Software vendors, consulting companies	CEBOS, OiWare, Nexum

Economic Trends

An understanding of economic trends is helpful in determining areas that are ripe for new business ideas as well as areas to avoid. When the economy is strong, people are more willing to buy discretionary products and services that enhance their lives. Individual sectors of the economy have a direct impact on consumer buying patterns. For example, a drop in interest rates typically leads to an increase in new home construction, furniture sales, and appliance sales. Conversely, a string of corporate lay-offs or a rapid decline in the stock market normally leads to a reduction in the demand for luxury goods such as expensive clothing and cars.

When studying how economic trends affect opportunities, it is important to evaluate who has money to spend and what they spend it on. For example, an increase in the number of women in the workforce and their related increase in disposable income is largely responsible for the number of clothing stores targeting professional women that have opened in the past several years. Some of the boutiques, like Ellen Tracey and Tory Burch, compete on a national scale, while others, like Olivine, in Seattle, are single-store boutiques that have been opened by an individual entrepreneur. There are also an increasing number of online stores that serve specific niche markets. For example, Shade Clothing is a realitvely new online store that designs and sells clothing for women who want apparel that is stylish yet not too revealing.

Similarly, as baby boomers reach retirement age, a sizeable portion of their spending will be redirected toward areas that make their retirement more comfortable, enjoyable, and secure. This trend will invariably spawn new businesses in many areas, largely because baby boomers have greater disposable income relative to previous generations. The most promising areas include finance, travel, housing, recreation, entertainment, and health care.

An understanding of economic trends can also help identify areas to avoid. For example, this is not a good time to start a company that relies on fossil fuels, such as airlines or trucking, because of high fuel prices. There are also certain product categories that suffer as a result of economic circumstances. This is not a good time to start a company that sells musical instruments, for example, such as violins, trumpets, and tubas. Domestic production of musical instruments has declined 3% annually over the past four years, and U.S. imports of musical instruments were down 7% from 2005 to 2006.[2] A major reason for this decline is that middle schools and high schools, which have historically been major buyers of musical instruments, have reduced their purchases due to budget cuts. In addition, the advent of online auction sites like eBay has made it easy for people to sell used musical instruments, which has cut into the market for new musical instrument sales.

Social Trends

An understanding of the impact of social trends on the way people live their lives and the products and services they need provides fertile ground for new business ideas. Often, the reason that a product or service exists has more to do with satisfying a social need than the more transparent need the product fills. For example, the proliferation of fast-food restaurants isn't due primarily to people's love for fast food but rather to the fact that people are busy and often don't have time to cook their own meals. Similarly, social networking sites such as MySpace and Facebook aren't popular because they can be used to post music and pictures on a Web site. They're popular because they allow people to connect and communicate with each other, which is a natural human tendency.

Changes in social trends alter how people and businesses behave and how they set their priorities. These changes affect how products and services are built and sold. A sample of the social trends that are currently affecting how individuals behave and set their priorities is provided here:

- Retirement of baby boomers
- The increasing diversity of the workforce
- Increasing interest in healthy foods and "green" products
- New forms of music and other types of entertainment
- The increasing focus on health care, fitness, and wellness
- Emphasis on alternative forms of energy
- Increasing globalization of business
- Increased purchasing power of women
- Increased purchasing power of teenagers and preteens
- Increased availability of inexpensive yet relatively powerful personal computers

Each of these trends is providing the impetus for new business ideas and will continue to do so. For example, the increasing emphasis on alternative forms of energy is spawning business ideas ranging from solar power, to wind-generated electricity, to alternatives for fossil fuels. One new company, Greasecar Vegetable Fuel Systems, makes conversion kits that allow diesel engines to run on vegetable oil. Justin Carvan, the company's founder, got interested in alternative fuels while at Hampshire College. The company is now growing at a rate of more than 200% per year and is projected to reach $2.5 million in annual sales shortly.[3] The increasing emphasis on green products is another social trend that is spawning interesting new business ideas. An example of a recent startup in this area is South West Trading Co., a business that specializes in earth-friendly, alternative fibers and textiles such as yarns made from bamboo, corn, and even recycled crab shells.

Technological Advances

Technological advances provide an ongoing source of new business ideas. In most cases, the technology itself isn't the key to recognizing business opportunities. Instead, the key is to recognize how technologies can be used and harnessed to help satisfy basic or changing human needs. For example, the creation of the cell phone is a technological achievement, but it was motivated by an increasingly mobile population that finds many advantages to having the ability to communicate with coworkers, customers, friends, and families from anywhere and everywhere.

Technological advancements also provide opportunities to help people perform everyday tasks in better or more convenient ways. For example, OpenTable.com is a Web site that allows users to make restaurant reservations online and now covers most of the United States. If you're planning a trip to San Francisco, for example, you can access OpenTable.com, select the area of the city you'll be visiting, and view descriptions, reviews, customer ratings, and in most cases the menus of the restaurants in the area. You can then make a reservation at the restaurant and print a map of directions. The basic tasks that OpenTable.com helps people perform have always been done— looking for a restaurant, comparing prices and menus, soliciting feedback from people who are familiar with competing restaurants, and getting directions. What OpenTable.com does is help people perform these takes in a more convenient and expedient manner.

Another aspect of technological advances is that once a technology is created, products often emerge to advance it. For example, the creation of the Apple iPod has created an entire industry that produces iPod accessories. An example is H2OAudio, a company that was started by four former San Diego State University students that makes waterproof housings for the iPod and the iPod nano. The waterproof housing permits iPod users to listen to their iPods while swimming, surfing, snowboarding, or engaging in any activity where the iPod is likely to get wet. There is a wide variety of other accessories available for the iPod, from designer cases to car rechargers. It is now estimated that for every $3 spent on an iPod, at least $1 is spent on an accessory.[4] Technology advances also give us new platforms to sell everyday products and services more efficiently and effectively. For example, at least four companies on the 2007 *Inc.* 500 started by selling their products on eBay.[5]

Political Action and Regulatory Changes

Political and regulatory changes also provide the basis for new business ideas. For example, new laws create opportunities for business owners to start firms to help companies, individuals, and governmental agencies comply with the laws. A case in point is the No Child Left Behind Act of 2002. The act, which is based on the notion of outcome-based education, requires states to develop criterion-based assessments in basic skills to be periodically given to all students in certain grades. Shortly after the act was passed, Kim and Jay Kleeman, two high school teachers, started Shakespeare Squared, a company that produces materials that help schools comply with the act. On some occasions, changes in government regulations motivate business owners to start firms that differentiate themselves by "exceeding" the regulation. For example, several years ago, the Federal Trade Commission changed the regulation about how far apart the wood or metal bars in an infant crib can be. If the bars are too far apart, a baby can get an arm or leg caught between the bars, causing an injury. A obvious business idea that might be spawned by this type of change is to produce a crib that is advertised and positioned as "exceeding" the new standard for width between bars and is "extra safe" for babies and young children. The change in regulation brings attention to the issue and provides ideal timing for a new company to reassure parents by providing a product that not only meets but exceeds the new regulation.

Political change also engenders new business and product opportunities. For example, global political instability and the threat of terrorism have resulted in many firms becoming more security conscious. These companies need new products and services to protect their physical assets and intellectual property as well as protect their customers and employees.

How Changing Environmental Trends Has Caused an Upswing in (of All Things) Mattress Sales

Some industries experience slow or no growth for years and experience sudden upswings in growth and popularity as the result of savvy industry incumbents or new business founders who realize that environmental change has turned in favor of the industry. In these instances, the businesses that pick up on these changes first and get out in front of the competition have an advantage. A recent example is the mattress industry. In *Business Week's* 2007 list of The Best (100) Small Companies to Watch, two of the companies, Select Comfort and Tempur-Pedic International, are mattress companies. Seriously, with all the high-tech and other interesting companies in the United States, would you have guessed that two mattress companies would have made the list? Probably not. But if you study the mattress industry, your sentiments will change. There are a number of significant environmental trends working in favor of the industry. These trends include:

- Rising incomes and a positive economic environment have led to increased mattress sales at the high end of the market.

- High shipping costs have limited imports from China and elsewhere (imports represent only 2.9% of U.S. mattress sales).

- The recent upswing in hotel and motel construction has resulted in a spike in mattress demand.

- There are roughly 2.7 million hospital and nursing home beds in the United States. These facilities typically purchase high-end mattresses with enhancements that allow them to be electronically adjusted. As the population ages, the healthcare market for mattresses will continue to grow.

- An increased emphasis on fitness and wellness has created new markets for mattresses that improve sleep quality and provide better neck and back support.

On Select Comfort and Tempur-Pedic's Web sites, you'll see that they're tapping into these exact trends. The broader U.S. mattress industry grew by 8.8% in 2004 and 6.9% in 2005, which are both impressive growth rates.

Unsolved Problems

The second approach to new business ideas is unsolved problems. Problems can be experienced or recognized by people through their jobs, hobbies, or everyday activities. Consistent with this observation, many companies have been started by people who have experienced a problem in their own lives, and in the process of solving the problem realized that they were on to a business idea. For example, in 2006 Christine Ingemi, a mother of four children under 11, became concerned by how loud her children were playing their MP3 players. She said she could hear music coming through her children's MP3 players' earphones when she was driving her van with the music on. To prevent her children from playing their MP3 players too loud, she and her husband, Rick, did some research, interviewed several audiologists, and invented a set of earbuds that limit the volume entering the user's ears. After her kids started using the earbuds, Ingemi began getting inquires from other parents asking where they could get a similar device. To make the device available to others, Ingemi started a business, called Ingemi Corp., to sell her IHearSafe earbuds.[6] Similarly, Laura Udall, another mother, invented an alternative to traditional backpacks when her fourth-grade daughter complained daily that her back hurt from carrying her backpack. After conducting research, obtaining feedback from student focus groups, and building several prototypes, Udall invented the ZUCA, a backpack on rollers that strikes the ideal balance between functionality and "cool" for kids. ZUCA is now a successful company, and its rolling backpacks can be purchased online or through a number of retailers.

Advances in technology often result in problems for people who can't use the technology in the way it is sold to the masses. For example, some older people find traditional cell phones hard to use—the buttons are small, the text is hard to read, and it's often difficult to hear someone on a cell phone in a noisy room. To solve these problems, GreatCall Inc., a recent startup, is producing a cell phone called the Jitterbug, which is designed specifically for older users. The Jitterbug features large buttons, easy-to-ready text, and a cushion that cups around the ear to improve sound quality. The phone also includes a button that connects the user directly with an operator who can assist in completing a call. Another company, Firefly Mobile, has created a cell phone designed specifically for tweens, ages 8 to 12. The phone only weighs two ounces and is designed to fit a kid's hand. The phone includes appropriate limitations for a young child and speed-dial keys for Mom and Dad.

A useful technique to use when confronted with a difficult problem is to find an instance where a similar issue was solved and then apply that solution to your problem. An example is provided by Susan Nichols, the founder of Yogitoes (www.yogitoes.com), a company that makes nonslip rugs for Yoga enthusiasts. Several Yoga positions require participants to strike poses where they balance their weight on their feet at an angle. In this position, it is easy to fall or slip when using a regular rug or mat. Nichols looked for a Yoga mat that would prevent her from slipping but found out that no one knew how to make one. So she started looking for an example of a product that was designed specifically to prevent it from slipping on a hard floor, to study how it functioned. Eventually, she stumbled upon a dog bowl with rubber nubs on the bottom to prevent it from sliding when a large dog ate or drank from it. Using the dog bowl (of all things) as a model, Nichols found a manufacturer who helped her develop a rug with small PVC nubs that prevent yoga participants from slipping when they perform Yoga moves. Nichols started Yogitoes to sell the rugs, and sales were on track to hit $3 million in 2006.[7]

Many other colorful examples of people who launched businesses to solve problems are included in Table 5.2.

Table 5.2   Companies Started to Solve a Problem

Business Founder	Year	Problem	Solution	Company That Resulted
Arlene Harris	2006	Many cell phones are too complicated, and the buttons are too small for seniors to use easily.	Designed a cell phone for seniors that is easy to use, has large buttons, and has a single button that when pushed connects to an operator who can assist with a call.	GreatCall
Scott Kliger	2006	411 directory assistance calls are expensive, costing from $1.25 to $3.75 per call, depending on the cellular provider.	Created a free, nation-wide, advertiser-supported, directory assistance service.	Jingle Networks

Business Founder	Year	Problem	Solution	Company That Resulted
David Bateman	2002	No way for apartment renters to pay their monthly rent online.	Created a software product that allows apartment complexes to enable their tenants to pay online.	Property Solutions
Lisa Druxman	2002	No fitness routine available to help new mothers stay fit and be with their newborns at the same time.	Created a franchise organization that promotes a workout routine (which involves a 45-minute power walk with strollers) that mothers and their babies can do together.	Stroller Stride
Richard Cole	1999	No service available to help people with computer problems at home.	Created an organization that makes "house calls" and helps people solve computer problems in their homes.	Geeks On Call

Gaps in the Marketplace

The third source of business ideas is gaps in the marketplace. There are many examples of products that consumers need or want, that aren't available in a particular location or aren't available at all. Part of the problem is created by large retailers, like Wal-Mart and Costco, which compete primarily on price and offer the most popular items targeted toward mainstream consumers. While this approach allows the large retailers to achieve economies of scale, it leaves gaps in the marketplace. This is the reason that clothing boutiques and specialty shops exist. These businesses are willing to carry merchandise that doesn't sell in large enough quantities for Wal-Mart or Costco to carry.

There are also product gaps in the marketplace, many of which represent potentially viable business opportunities. For example, in 1997, Julie Aigner-Clark realized that there were no videos on the market to expose her one-year old daughter to music, the arts, and science. To fill this gap, she started Baby Einstein, a company that produced uplifting videos for children aged three months to three years. The company did so well that it was acquired by Disney in 2001. A more common example of a company that filled a gap in the marketplace is provided by p.45 (www.p45.com), a women's clothing boutique in Chicago. The store carries innovative collections from young fashion designers, original pieces of jewelry made by Chicago area residents, unique shoes, and accessories that complement the clothing in the store. p.45 fills a gap in the marketplace by offering people with particular tastes a line of clothing and accessories that they couldn't find in mainstream stores. It is also located in an area of Chicago that has a sufficient critical mass of upscale shoppers to support the store.

A common way that gaps in the marketplace are recognized is when people become frustrated because they can't find a product or service that they need and recognize that other people feel the same frustration. This scenerio played out for Lorna Ketler and Barb Wilkins, who became frustrated when they couldn't find stylish "plus-sized" clothing that fit. In response to their frustration, they started Bodacious (www.bodacious.ca), a store that sells fun and stylish clothing for hard-to-fit women. Ketler and Wilkins' experience illustrates how compelling a business idea can be when it strikes just the right cord by filling a gap that deeply resonates with a specific clientele. Reflecting on the success of Bodacious, Wilkins said:

> *"It's so rewarding when you take a risk and it pays off for you and people are telling you every single day, 'I'm so glad you're here.' We've had people cry in our store. It happens a lot. They're crying because they're so happy (that they're finding clothes that fit). One woman put on a pair of jeans that fit her, and she called me an hour later and said, 'They still look good, even at home!' Sometimes people have a body change that happens, whether they have been ill or had a baby, and there's lots of emotion involved in it. If you can go out and buy clothes that fit, that helps people feel good about themselves."*[8]

A related technique for generating new business ideas is to take an existing product or service and create a new category by targeting a completely different target market. This approach essentially involves creating a gap and filling it. An example is PopCap games (www.popcap.com), a company that was started to create a new category in the electronic games industry called "casual games." The games are casual and relaxing rather than flashy and action-packed and are made for people who want to wind down after a busy day. Currently, 90% of the company's customers are women 25 years old or older, which is a completely different demographic than the young males that the mainstream game manufacturers target.[9] Another approach to filling gaps in the marketplace is to service an area that is lacking a particular product or service. For example, SPC Office Products (www.spcop.com) is a company that sells the same products as Staples and Office Depot but focuses on towns under 20,000 in population. As a rule of thumb, SPC doesn't like to open a store that's within 120 miles of a Staples or Office Depot.[10]

Other examples of companies that were launched to fill gaps in the marketplace are included in Table 5.3.

Table 5.3 Companies Started to Fill a Gap in the Marketplace

Gap in the Marketplace	Resulting New Business Opportunity	Companies That Resulted
No fitness centers designed specifically for women.	Created a fitness center that is just for women, features workouts and exercise machines designed specifically for women, and fits the time and budgetary constraints of its female clientele.	Curves, Contours Express, Lady of America
Lack of toys that focus on the intellectual development of a child.	Toy stores, direct-sales organizations (like Tupperware), and Web sites that sell educational toys.	Discovery Toys, Kazoo & Company
No hair care, skin care, and body care stores that are fresher and more sophisticated than standard Bath and Body outlets but less upscale than high-end stores like Nordstrom's and Sacks.	Specialty boutiques that offer fresh, new, natural, and organic hair care, skin care, and body care products.	Aveda, Origins, Sephora

continues

Table 5.3   Continued

Gap in the Marketplace	Resulting New Business Opportunity	Companies That Resulted
Restaurants that are both fast and serve good food.	Fast-casual restaurants that combine the advantages of fast-food (fast service) and casual dining (good food).	Panera Bread, Chipotle, Cosi
Shortage of clothing stores that sell fashionable clothing for hard-to-fit people.	Boutiques that sell fashionable clothing for hard-to-fit people—which may include plus-sized clothes, maternity clothes, or clothing for tall or short people.	Casual Male, Ashley Stewart, Casual Plus

Techniques for Generating Ideas

Most businesses are started in one of two ways. Some businesses are internally stimulated. An individual, who hadn't necessarily been thinking about starting a business, sees a problem or recognizes a gap in the marketplace and creates a business to fill it. This was the case with Laura Udall of ZUCA as well as Julie Aigner-Clark of Baby Einstein, who were discussed earlier. Other businesses are externally stimulated. In this instance, an individual has a strong interest in starting a business and then starts looking for ideas for businesses to start. This was the case with Jeff Bezos, the founder of Amazon.com. In 1994, Bezos quit his lucrative job at a New York City investment firm and headed for Seattle with a plan to find an attractive opportunity and launch an e-commerce firm. After kicking around a number of different ideas, he settled on books and started Amazon.com.

This section of the chapter focuses on two techniques that people use to try to explicitly generate new business ideas. These techniques are most commonly used by people searching for business ideas but are also used by people who spot an opportunity (like Laura Udall did when she realized that her daughter needed a different kind of backpack) and want to flesh-out their ideas. Having knowledge about each of the three most common sources of business ideas, articulated here, enhances each of these techniques.

One point to remain mindful of while considering these techniques is that business ideas take time to develop, so it's important not to become discouraged if an idea doesn't surface quickly. It's also important to realize that the best ideas aren't necessarily the most original—as long as the idea is "different" enough that it adds unique value for the consumer. As mentioned earlier in the chapter, it normally exceeds the budget of a new firm to educate the public about a revolutionary or completely original idea.

Why the Most Original Ideas Aren't Always the Best Ideas

When considering business ideas, it's important to realize that the best ideas aren't always the most original ones, as indicated at the beginning of the chapter. New firms don't often have the capital to effectively get their names and products or services quickly recognizable.

The diagram pictured here provides a quick visual depiction of the four categories of new business ideas and the most realistic categories for new firms. The simplest ideas (existing products in existing markets) are located in Box 1 and are generally undesirable because they are in crowded fields with stiff competition. The trickiest and most expensive to implement ideas are in Box 4 (new products in new markets) and are usually avoided because they put a new firm too far out on a limb. The most practical ideas for most new businesses are located in either Box 2 or Box 3. The vast majority of new businesses referred to in this book are Box 2 or Box 3 startups.[11]

	Existing Products	New Products
Existing Markets	1	2
New Markets	3	4

Brainstorming

The term *brainstorming* is a catch phrase that means different things to different people. In general, brainstorming is simply the process of generating several ideas about a specific topic. It can easily be used to generate business ideas. The approaches range from a person sitting down with a yellow legal pad and jotting down interesting business ideas to formal "brainstorming sessions" led by moderators that involve a group of people.

In a formal brainstorming session, the leader of the group asks the participants to share their ideas. One person shares an idea, another person reacts to it, another person reacts to the reaction, and so on. A flip chart or whiteboard is typically used to record the ideas. A productive brainstorming session is freewheeling and lively. The session is not used for analysis or decision-making—the ideas generated during a brainstorming session need to be filtered and analyzed, but this is done later. The number one rule of a brainstorming session is that no criticism is allowed, including chuckles, raised eyebrows, or facial expressions that express skepticism or doubt. Criticism stymies creativity and inhibits the free flow of ideas.

Brainstorming sessions dedicated to generating new business ideas are often less formal. For example, during the creation of Proactiv, a popular acne treatment product, Dr. Katie Rodan, one of the company's founders, hosted dinner parties at her house and conducted brainstorming sessions with guests. The guests included business executives, market researchers, marketing consultants, the chief financial officer of a major company, an FDA regulatory attorney, and others. Rodan credits this group with helping her and her cofounder brainstorm a number of ideas that helped shape the company and move the process of starting the company along.[12] Similarly, Sharelle Klause, the founder of Dry Soda, a company that makes an all-natural soda that's paired with food the way wine is in upscale restaurants, tested her idea by first talking to her husband's colleagues, who were in the food industry, and then tapped into the professional network of a friend who owned a bottled water company. Through this process she met a chemist, who was instrumental in helping her develop the initial recipes for her beverage. Klause also went directly to restaurant owners and chefs to ask them to sample early versions of her product.[13] While this approach only loosely fits the definition of brainstorming, the spirit is the same. Klause was bouncing ideas and early prototypes of her product off others to get their reactions and generate additional ideas.

Approaches to brainstorming are only limited by your imagination. For example, to teach her students an approach to utilizing brainstorming to generate business ideas, Marcene Sonneborn, an adjunct professor in the Whitman School of Management at Syracuse University, uses a tool she developed called the "bug report" to help her students brainstorm business ideas. She instructs her students to list 75 things that "bug" them in their everyday lives. The number 75 was chosen because it forces students to go beyond thinking about obvious things that bug them (campus parking, roommates, scraping snow off their windshields in the winter), and think more deeply. On occasion, students actually hold focus groups with their friends to brainstorm ideas and fill out their lists. Another particularly effective approach to brainstorming is to utilize the three sources for new business ideas as a way of organizing the discussion. Imagine this: Suppose you are part of a small group that is trying to brainstorm ideas for a new type of fitness center. You know the market is too crowded to support another generic center, so you're looking for novel ideas. You create three columns on a whiteboard labeled Changing Environmental Trends, Unsolved Problems, and Gaps in the Marketplace. You then start brainstorming specific ideas, looking at each category individually, and then at how the categories interact with each other. After brainstorming dozens of ideas in each category, you start grouping the ideas into themes or patterns to create more solid ideas. One pattern jumps out at you: The population is aging, older people are increasingly interested in fitness, many of the exercise machines and classes taught in traditional fitness centers aren't suitable for older people, and there are no fitness centers designed specifically for the 50+ demographic. Based on this pattern, your first solid idea is to create a fitness center designed specifically for people 50 years old and older.

Library and Internet Research

A second approach people can use to generate new business ideas is to conduct library and Internet research, as discussed briefly in Chapter 2. A natural tendency is to think that an idea should be chosen, and the process of researching the idea should then begin. This approach is too linear. Often, the best ideas emerge when the general notion of an idea, like opening an innovative type of fitness center, is merged with extensive library and Internet research, which might provide insights into the best type of innovative fitness center to pursue.

Libraries are often an underutilized source of information for generating business ideas, as mentioned earlier in the book. The best approach to utilizing a library is to discuss your general area of interest with a reference librarian, who can point out useful resources, such as powerful online resources that libraries often have access to. An example is Mintel, an online resource that publishes market research on all major industries and sub-categories within industries. Mintel has literally dozens of pages of information on the "Health and Fitness Club" industry alone. Spending time reading through the information could spark new ideas for fitness centers or help affirm an existing idea. Just a few minutes reading Mintel's report bodes well for the idea of opening a fitness center for the 50+ demographic. According to the report, while 45% of people say they exercise regularly, only 22% belong to fitness clubs, which suggests there are opportunities for membership growth. Households with higher incomes are more likely to belong to fitness clubs, which fits the 50+ demographic. Individuals who are 35 to 54 are the most likely candidates to join health clubs. Interestingly, 67% of the people who currently don't belong to a fitness club said they would join if they knew the activities would keep them motivated. Mintel's summary of the fitness club industry concluded by stating, "It is important for health clubs to tailor their offerings to their target market."[14] This is exactly what a fitness center for the 50+ demographic would do. Equally insightful information is available for all industries, so it might be a good use of your time to visit a university or large city library to access the Mintel report on your area of interest.

Internet research is also important. If you're starting from scratch, simply type "new business ideas" into Google or Yahoo!, and it will produce links to newspaper and magazine articles about the "hottest" and "latest" new business ideas. While these types of articles are general in nature, they provide a starting point if you're trying to generate new business ideas from scratch. If you have a specific idea in mind, like the fitness center concept we've been discussing, a useful technique is to set up a Google or Yahoo "email alert" using keywords that pertain to your topic of interest. Google and Yahoo! alerts are email updates of the latest Google or Yahoo! results (i.e., Web site updates, press releases, news articles, blog postings) based on your topic. This technique, which is available for free, will feed you a daily stream of news articles and blog postings about specific topics.

Summary

The ability to generate a good business idea is a key ingredient to launching a successful startup. Many businesses fail not because the people involved weren't committed or didn't work hard; they fail because the businesses weren't good ideas to start with. Don't let this happen to you. Following the frameworks and suggestions provided in this chapter can help you enhance your chances of coming up with a business idea that is successful.

The next chapter deals with the myth that no one can compete against Wal-Mart and the other big-box retailers. This myth is true in part—virtually no one can compete against big-box retailers at their own game. New businesses can compete if they understand what the big-boxes' strengths and vulnerabilities are and adjust their strategies accordingly.

Endnotes

1 Philip Kotler, *Marketing Insights from A to Z* (New York: John Wiley & Sons, 2003), 128.

2 First Research, 2007.

3 S. Cooper and others, "The Hot List," Entrepreneur.com, December, 2006.

4 Damon Darlin, "The iPod Ecosystem," *The New York Times*, February 3, 2006.

5 *"Inc. 500," Inc.*, September 2007, 77.

6 K. Spiller, "Low-Decibel Earbuds Keep Noise At a Reasonable Level," *The Nashua Telegraph*, August 13, 2006.

7 "A Foothold in the Yoga Market," *Business 2.0*, July 2006, 64.

8 Ladies Who Launch, accessed October 4, 2007 (see chap. 1, n. 4).

9 nPost, accessed October 4, 2007 (see chap. 1, n. 11).

10 Bailey, J., "How One Small Store Thrives Among Giants," Startup Journal home page, http://www.startupjournal.com.

11 "Getting New Business Ideas," Adapted from PlanWare, http://www.planware.org, accessed September 1, 2007.

12 K. Rodan, "Entrepreneurial Thought Leaders" Podcast, Stanford Technology Ventures, http://stvp.stanford.edu/, April 2006.

13 Greg Galant and Sharelle Klause, "VV Show #35," Venture Voice: Entertaining Entrepreneurship, http://www.venturevoice.com, March 2006.

14 Mintel, 2007.

PART II

Running and Growing a Business—
Don't Underestimate Your Chances

CHAPTER 6

Myth No. 6:
No One Can Compete Against Wal-Mart
and the Other Big-Box Retailers

Truth No. 6:
You Can Compete Against the Big-Box
Retailers if You Have the Right Plan

Introduction

One of the main fears that many prospective business owners have is whether they'll be able to compete against Wal-Mart, Home Depot, Best Buy, and the other big-box retailers. It's a legitimate fear. The big-box stores continue to grow, not only in terms of size but in terms of geographic breadth and product line. There are now big-box stores in towns as small as 10,000 people. And the stores don't just sell goods; they sell services, too. For example, Home Depot sells installation services for the carpet it carries, and Best Buy offers at-home computer training and repair. There are also anecdotes, which all of us have heard, of big-box stores moving into towns and driving local merchants out of business. If established businesses can't compete against Wal-Mart or Home Depot, it's hard to blame a prospective business owner for worrying about whether his or her business will have any chance at all.

The reality, though, is that despite these obstacles, many small businesses do compete successfully against big-box retailers. Their success, however, is not by chance. While it's nearly impossible to compete against Wal-Mart and the others on price, price isn't everything. There are many other forms of competition including product quality, customer service, product knowledge, convenience, ties to the local community, and so on. The businesses that compete successfully against the big-box retailers compete on one or more of these variables and avoid head-to-head competition on price. They also manage their businesses prudently and employ steps to keep their costs in check and to get the word out about the points of differentiation between their businesses and the big guys.

The purpose of this chapter is to more fully explore this important topic. In our view, the notion that no one can compete against Wal-Mart and the other big-box retailers is a myth—but there is a caveat attached. In general, no one can compete against the big-box retailers at their own game. So, if you're thinking about starting a business that will compete against a big-box retailer (and most businesses do at some level), you have to first understand their game and then develop a strategy and set of tactics that gives people reason to do business with you. In our experience, the big-box retailers are vulnerable but only to businesses that have a firm sense of how to compete against them.

This chapter proceeds in the following manner. First, we describe how the big-box retailers compete and what their vulnerabilities are. Although Wal-Mart, Home Depot, Costco, and the others are different in many ways, their overall strategies and vulnerabilities are similar. Second, we describe the three most common approaches employed by businesses that compete successfully against the big-box stores. Third, we lay out two specific tactics that new businesses use to make these approaches successful.

How Big-Box Retailers Compete and What Their Vulnerabilities Are

There are two categories of big-box retailers. The first are the general merchandise stores, such as Wal-Mart, Kmart, Costco, and BJ's Wholesale Club. These are the biggest stores, ranging from 50,000 to 225,000 square feet. The second are the category killers, such as Home Depot, Best Buy, PetSmart, Dick's Sporting Goods, and Bed Bath & Beyond. These stores focus on a single category and offer a wide selection of merchandise in that category. The name "big-box" comes from the physical appearance of the stores. They are normally large, free-standing, rectangular, single-floor stores on a concrete slab.

How the Big-Box Retailers Compete

The general merchandise stores, such as Wal-Mart and Target, compete primarily on price and selection. Although they attract people from all income levels, their most frequent customers are people in middle- and lower-income categories. The stores advertise "everyday low prices" and "one-stop shopping" and carry a wide selection of merchandise, from clothing and electronics to prescription drugs, food, toys, and automotive supplies. A Wal-Mart SuperCenter features up to 142,000 items. The approaches of the stores vary some. Costco and Sam's Club, for example, target small business owners along with the general public. Costco features a smattering of high quality products, such as Godiva chocolate and Waterford crystal, at bargain prices. Target has differentiated itself within the general merchandise big-box category by featuring more attractive stores with a slightly higher quality mix of merchandise.

The category killers follow much the same strategy but focus on a single category, such as electronics, pet supplies, sporting goods, or toys. While a category killer store, such as Best Buy or PetSmart, is not as large as a Wal-Mart or Costco, the advantage they have is an ability to zero in on a single category and provide better product knowledge. By focusing on a single category, the category killers are also able to generate more passion among their customers than the general merchandise stores.

Behind the scenes, the lower prices the big-box stores offer are made possible by volume sales, supply chain efficiencies, aggressive negotiations with vendors, and low overhead. The big-box concept also relies on Wal-Mart's original notion of "value loop" retailing as shown in Figure 6.1. The basic idea behind value loop retailing is that low prices generate healthy sales and profits. If a portion of the profits are reinvested in still lower prices, the prices will generate still higher sales and profits. If a portion of these profits are reinvested in still lower prices, sales and profits will continue to rise and so on and so on.[1] There is, of course, a limit to how much sales can go up and prices can go down, but it's easy to see the gist of the strategy.

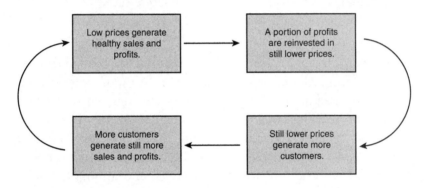

Figure 6.1   *Key to big-box retailers' success: Value loop pricing*

Along with low prices and a broad selection, the big-box stores also pursue a saturation strategy. Wal-Mart has literally blanketed the country with over 1,075 Wal-Mart discount stores, 2,250 Wal-Mart SuperCenter's, 580 Sam's Clubs, and a growing number of Wal-Mart Neighborhood Markets. Target now has over 1,500 stores, and Costco has 490. In the category killer group, Home Depot has 1,900 stores, Best Buy has 820, PetSmart has 900, and Beth Bath & Beyond has 815. These stores are not confined to urban areas. As mentioned earlier, Wal-Mart now has SuperCenters in towns as small as 10,000 in population, and the other big-box retailers are following suit. In most parts of the country, consumers have several big-box stores in their immediate shopping areas.

Vulnerabilities of the Big-Box Stores

The big-box stores have several vulnerabilities. The general merchandisers feature a product strategy that is a mile wide and an inch deep, which limits their ability to provide a wide selection of products or superior product knowledge in any one area. The basic idea is to sell the most popular products in as many categories as possible to value-minded consumers. While this approach allows the general merchandisers to achieve economies of scale (think of how many bottles of Tide Wal-Mart sells in a day), it leaves gaps in the marketplace, as explained in Chapter 5. The general merchandise stores are also vulnerable in regard to customer service, product knowledge, and their ability to develop one-on-one relationships with customers. The very nature of Wal-Mart, Kmart, and Costco's low-cost approach limits the amount they're willing to invest in customer service, and the sheer number of products they sell makes an intimate knowledge of each product impossible. The large size of their stores is also wearisome for many shoppers, who tire of crowded aisles, long checkout lines, an inability to find what they're looking for, and the lack of assistance when needed.

The same vulnerabilities that apply to the general merchandise stores apply to the category killers to a slightly lesser degree. Although the category killers, like Home Depot and PetSmart, are generally better at customer service and product knowledge than the general merchandise stores, they're still trying to sell the most popular products to mainstream consumers, which leaves gaps in the marketplace for others to fill. For example, Dick's Sporting Goods offers an impressive selection of sporting goods and apparel, but it can't offer everything. This reality provides an opening for a company like Just For Girls Sports, which is an online store that specializes in products that are especially designed for athletic girls, teens, and women. The category killer stores are also subject to the same criticism that general merchandise stores experience as a result of their size. While some people enjoy browsing around a large store like a Best Buy or a Dick's Sporting Goods, other people find the experience irritating and tiring.

A vulnerability that applies to both categories of big-box stores, which is most pronounced when a Wal-Mart or a Home Depot enters a smaller town, is a lack of ties to the local community and a perception that the larger store is a threat to local merchants. This issue has resulted in town meetings across the country as local communities have wrestled with the pluses and minuses of allowing big-box retailers to locate in their towns. While big-box stores provide employment and offer consumers access to lower-priced products, they also impact local businesses and take money out of a community. Both of these latter points have been affirmed by careful studies. A study conducted by Kenneth Stone, an Iowa State University economist, found that in the 10 years after a Wal-Mart opened, general-merchandise sales in Iowa towns with a Wal-Mart rose by 25% (mostly from Wal-Mart), while general-merchandise sales in surrounding towns dropped by 34%. During the same period, sales for both clothing stores and specialty stores dropped by 15% to 28% in both Wal-Mart towns and surrounding communities.[2] Similarly, economic impact studies have found that a much lower percentage of money spent at a chain store stays in the local community opposed to money spent at a locally owned business. A study conducted in the Andersonville district of North Chicago found that $68 of every $100 spent at a local firm stayed in the Chicago area while only $43 of every $100 spent in a chain store stayed in the community.[3]

The upshot of this discussion is potentially heartening for prospective business owners. While the big-box retailers clearly win on price, and to lesser degree on selection, they are vulnerable on product quality, product knowledge, customer service, convenience, ties to the local community, and other variables. Because they can't carry everything, they also leave gaps in the marketplace, providing the opportunity for other businesses to fill them. Luckily for new businesses, because the big-box retailers compete primarily at the low end of the market on price, the gaps they leave are generally at the high end of the market where profit margins are larger. Several of the businesses discussed in this book fit this description, including Wadee (handmade children's toys), J.J. Creations (designer bags and backpacks), and Real Cosmetics (skin care products for women of all nationalities). These businesses sell higher-margin products that don't fit the traditional product mix of a big-box retailer.

Table 6.1 illustrates the impact of this collection of insights on a potential new business. Imagine you are thinking about opening a nursery to sell plants, shrubs, trees, and lawn and garden supplies, but are hesitant to move forward because Wal-Mart and Home Depot are in your area and are selling similar products. Assuming that you're knowledgeable, willing to provide a high level of customer service, willing to promote the idea that you're a locally owned company, and otherwise capable of running a sound business, the checklist here shows the areas in which you can win and the areas that you'll most likely lose in competition with Wal-Mart and Home Depot. As shown in the table, while Wal-Mart and Home Depot will invariably win on price and selection might be a draw, you can potentially win every other category (and serve customers that find these categories important). This is the general circumstance in which new firms and existing businesses compete successfully against big-box retailers.

Table 6.1 Garden Nursery Versus Wal-Mart and Home Depot

Point of Competition	Advantage—Wal-Mart and Home Depot	Advantage—Small/ New Business
Price	X	
Selection	draw	draw
Product quality		X
Product knowledge		X
Customer service		X
Convenience		X
Ties to local community		X

The next section of this chapter talks about the three most common approaches employed by small businesses to compete successfully against big-box retailers.

Approaches for Competing Successfully Against Big-Box Retailers

There are many lessons those wanting to start their own businesses can learn from existing firms about competing successfully against big-box retailers. The primary lesson is to take the threat seriously and not leave things to chance. If you plan to open a store or sell products or services that will compete directly against a big-box retailer, you should have an explicit strategy for dealing with the big-box threat. Small businesses don't always do this. A pattern researchers have noticed in retailers that go out of business when a Wal-Mart or other big-box store comes to town is they don't adjust their strategies. In fact, one study of 62 small retailers in southwestern Virginia found that 52% of store keepers didn't adjust their product lineup, 42% didn't adjust their pricing, and 21% didn't adjust their service levels when a Wal-Mart opened in their area.

Another way of looking at the big-box phenomenon is that there are many businesses that it benefits. Local businesses often supply products and services to help the big-boxes operate. In addition, if your business offers a product line that complements rather than competes against a big-box retailer you might actually benefit by locating it in close proximity to the larger store. This strategy is pursued by Sally Beauty Supply, which appears in 26% of U.S. Wal-Mart anchored shopping centers. Explaining the rationale behind this strategy, Sally Beauty Supply spokeswoman Jan Roberts said:

> *"Wal-Mart generates an enormous amount of traffic, and we like to feed off that. We do have a few similar products, but we offer much more selection. If someone is looking for specific beauty items, we are more likely to have them...like the 400 (personal) appliances we carry, such as blow-dryers and curling irons."*[4]

Now let's look at the three most common approaches that small businesses utilize to compete against big-box retailers.

Operate in a Niche Market

As mentioned in Chapter 5, a niche market is a place within a larger market segment that represents a narrower group of customers with similar needs. It's normally smart for a business that will compete against a big-box retailer to operate in a niche market so it can position itself as a "specialist" and provide a compelling reason for customers to shop at its store. This is what Sally Beauty Supply has done. It offers a very deep line of one product—beauty supplies. As a result of this singular focus, it can position itself as the "place to shop" for beauty supplies in a local community.

This same philosophy can be pursued in virtually any product category, as long as there are enough potential customers to support the business. An example is Paige's Music in Indianapolis. The company, which has been in business since 1871, sells musical instruments to school bands and orchestras. The musical instrument industry is a tough industry, as mentioned in Chapter 5, and sales are down nationwide for a variety of reasons. Competition is also intense. Wal-Mart and Costco sell musical instruments, and there are several national musical instrument chains, including Guitar Center and Sam Ash Music. Despite these threats, Paige's Music continues to grow, largely because of its laser focus on selling to school bands and orchestras, which is a niche market. "There are plenty of opportunities for the small local store to succeed against the big boys," says Mark Goff, owner and president of Paige's Music, "but you've got to hit 'em where they ain't."[5] Paige's primary market is the 400 school bands and orchestras in Indiana, along with the 36,000 students who are enrolled in music classes in Indiana schools. The store's salespeople regularly call on the band and orchestra directors they sell to. This is a tactic that will most likely never be matched by Wal-Mart, Costco, or one of the national musical instrument chains.

If the business or store you're contemplating will have some of the characteristics of a general merchandiser or category killer, you can still benefit by serving niche markets within the context of a larger business. For instance, in the example of the prospective nursery provided earlier, along with competing against Wal-Mart and Home Depot on factors other than price, the nursery could also become a specialist in one or more areas. For example, it might "specialize" in providing hedges, shrubbery, and sod for new construction and try to develop relationships with local builders and contractors. This is a niche market within the larger lawn and garden supply industry. It might also become the "place to go to" to purchase outdoor or indoor fountains. The overall point is that if the nursery couples its focus on the potential points of advantage along with becoming a specialist in one or two areas (while still selling its entire line of products), it will enhance its chances of success.

Differentiate

Once a business selects a niche market, it must differentiate itself from larger stores that sell similar products. Selecting a niche market, such as indoor and outdoor fountains or beauty supplies, is only the first step in separating your business from your larger rivals. The second step is to create meaningful forms of differentiation. Sally Beauty Supply relies on depth of product line and product knowledge as its forms of differentiation. Anyone who has shopped at Wal-Mart and Sally's knows that Sally's has a much broader and deeper line of beauty supplies. This doesn't mean that everyone will buy their beauty supplies from Sally's. But Sally's provides people who want a larger selection of beauty supplies to choose from, a clear alternative to Wal-Mart. The biggest mistake that new firms and existing businesses make when trying to compete against big-box retailers is not drawing a sharp enough contrast between what they have to offer and what the big-box stores have. This notion is affirmed by Kenneth Stone, the Iowa State University economist mentioned earlier in the chapter. After spending 12 years studying the impact of the entry of Wal-Mart stores on small communities in Iowa, Stone concluded that businesses that adjusted and offered something different than Wal-Mart actually benefited from the spillover of additional traffic, while businesses that sold items similar to Wal-Mart lost sales unless they repositioned themselves.[6]

The primary thing to be mindful of in planning a differentiation strategy is the need to differentiate along lines that are important to customers. Apparently, depth of product line and product knowledge are important to Sally's Beauty Supply customers, as evidenced by Sally's success. Another example is Sam's Wine & Spirits, a wine and liquor store that is sandwiched among a Costco, Cost Plus, Trader Joe's, and Whole Foods in Chicago. To compete against its big-box rivals, Sam's Wine & Spirits stresses customer service, product selection, product knowledge, and education. The education piece is the most interesting. To deepen its relationship with its customers, the company has created Sam's Academy, which offers adult education classes (on wine and liquor), wine tasting experiences, and reward programs for repeat customers. Explaining the rationale for these initiatives, Brian Rosen, one of the business's owners said, "(Wine) is a knowledge-driven subject, and people want to be educated." Again, the beauty of this form of differentiation is that it's unlikely to be mimicked by one of Sam's Wine & Spirit's big-box rivals.

There are many other ways to differentiate a small business from larger rivals. Some businesses seek out employees who speak the language of their customers—literally. For example, Wheelworks, a large bicycle store in Belmont, Massachusetts (which is near Boston), employs people who speak Spanish, French, Italian, Chinese, and several other languages. This aspect of Wheelwork's business fits the ethnically diverse nature of its community and provides it an advantage over stores that aren't as sensitive to this issue. Other companies, like locally owned office supply stores, offer free delivery, day or night, which is something that a Costco, Office Max, or Staples is unlikely to do. Probably the most important form of differentiation is customer service. While almost all companies tout customer service as a point of differentiation, small businesses are able to deliver it in unique ways. For example, remembering the names of frequent customers, writing thank you notes for large orders, and knowing customers' buying habits is something that small businesses are uniquely capable of doing.

One final note that is particularly encouraging for new or small businesses is that there is growing evidence that price, the factor the big-box retailers rely on the most, might be a fairly fragile form of differentiation. According to the *Harvard Business Review*, two-thirds of shoppers find the entire Wal-Mart shopping experience not worth the savings.[7] A recent *Wall Street Journal* article affirmed this sentiment by reporting that specialty retailers across all segments are gaining on Wal-Mart despite Wal-Mart's price advantages.[8]

Kazoo & Company: You Can Compete Against the Big Guys—If You Have the Right Plan

There is no denying it. There are many challenges in competing against big-box retailers. So how is it that Kazoo & Company, an independent toy store in Denver, Colorado, is thriving? It's thriving because of two things—the business has a doggedly determined owner at the helm, and it has a good plan. After you read this short account, you'll nod you head and think to yourself, yup—that's a good plan.

Diana Nelson bought Kazoo & Company in 1998. From the outset, she had no illusions that owing a toy store would be easy. When she bought Kazoo, independent toy stores were being tattered to pieces by Wal-Mart, Toys "R" Us, and other large retailers. So she knew the only way to beat them was to outthink them. This is how she did it.

Nelson decided to differentiate Kazoo & Company from Wal-Mart, Toys "R" Us, and other large toy retailers on five specific dimensions.

First, the store changed its merchandise mix. Nelson replaced the Mattel, Crayola, and Fisher-Price toys (which could be bought anywhere) with unique items such as Gotz Dolls from Germany and a wide range of educational toys.

Second, the store welcomes professionals, like speech therapists, to bring their patients into the store to play with them and identify specific toys that might help them progress in their treatments. Observing professionals work with their patients (that is, young children who have some type of disability) also helps Kazoo & Company's staff know what to recommend when a parent comes in looking for a similar solution.

Third, Kazoo's store design is unique. While the store itself is still fairly small, it is further broken down into smaller, more intimate departments.

Fourth, the company focuses intently on customer service. This facet of Kazoo's operation is particularly apparent in its e-commerce site, which was initiated in 1999. As evidence of this, the following comment was posted recently on a Yahoo! bulletin board site, where a consumer wrote a comment about his experience shopping at Kazoo.com:

"Old-fashioned friendly service. When I called to check on the delivery date of a little piano I had ordered for my grandson, I was actually speaking to a person that was friendly, polite, courteous, and just delightful. I will continue to buy from this company. They have a real interest in giving top-quality service. It has been a most enjoyable experience."

Fifth, the inventory in the store is freshened up frequently, so regular customers see different toys each time they come into the store.

Kazoo's plan and its sharp execution have paid off. Business is growing, and the company has been selected by the Toy Industry Association as one of the Top 5 Specialty Retail Toy Stores in North America several times since it was purchased by Diana Nelson.[9]

Stress "Locally Owned"

A third approach that businesses use to compete successfully against big-box retailers is to stress the locally owned facet of their businesses (if they are locally-owned). This approach tugs at the heart strings of people who are loyal to their local communities and have a natural inclination to want to see local businesses succeed. The strategy is evident in signs that are placed in store windows or in ads that read "Locally Owned Business," "We Sell Locally Made Jewelry," or other similar comments. In fact, this type of strategy is much more than an advertising gimmick. One study of residents in Maine, New Hampshire, and Vermont found that 17% to 40% of consumers in each state were willing to pay two dollars more to buy a locally produced $5.00 food item.[10] Similarly, a study by the Leopold Center for Sustainable Agriculture found that "grown locally" ranked significantly higher than "organic" in regard to consumer preferences for fresh produce and meats.[11]

Stressing the local nature of a business can also be helpful in building its brand. Many states and regions of the country have placed labels on products originating from their geographic areas to draw attention to their wholesomeness and freshness. Examples include "Tennessee Pride," "Jersey Fresh," and "Iowa Beef." The subtle message conveyed by these labels is not only where the products come from but where they don't come from. For example, most consumers would probably prefer "Alaskan Wild Salmon" to salmon advertised as coming from a densely populated fish farm in Chile (which is where most salmon in the United States comes from). While the Chilean salmon might be perfectly fine, the freshness factor and the U.S. roots of the Alaskan salmon are likely to give it a leg up for most American consumers.

The same philosophy can be applied at an individual business level. A locally owned business can tout the wholesomeness and freshness of its products (if applicable) as effectively as a region or state. It can also draw attention to the positive economic impact that locally owned businesses have on a community or local economy.

Specific Tactics That Local Businesses Use to Support Their Independent Status

There are a number of tactics that new and small businesses use to support the general approaches described here and to maintain their independently owned status. A tactic is a method employed to help achieve a certain goal. While most companies have similar broad strategic goals (increasing sales, increasing profits, producing quality products, behaving in an ethical manner, and so on), the ways in which they achieve their goals vary widely. The two tactics shown in the following sections are most applicable to businesses that plan to remain independently owned and are particularly concerned about competing against big-box retailers.

Partner with Other Small Businesses

A common tactic new businesses employ is to partner with other new or small businesses to increase their clout and buying power. Making this happen takes initiative and pre-planning on the part of a prospective business owner. He or she must get to know other business owners and establish relationships before the business is started.

There are several ways that small businesses can partner with one another in an effort to be as competitive in the marketplace as possible. One way is by joining or organizing buying groups or co-ops, where small businesses band together to attain volume discounts on products and services. An example is Intercounty Appliance, a buying co-op for 85 independent appliance stores in the Northeast. The co-op aggregates the purchasing power of its members to get volume discounts on appliances and other items such as flat-screen plasma TVs. An example of a much larger buying co-op is the Independent Pharmacy Cooperative, which was founded in Madison, Wisconsin in 1984. It has since grown into the nation's largest purchase organization for independent pharmacies with over 3,200 member stores and is one of the major reasons that independent pharmacies are able to compete against Walgreens and CVS. There are similar buying co-ops in other industries. In many cases, the co-ops can get the same pricing on merchandise from a vendor as a big-box retailer. While belonging to a buying co-op doesn't mean an independent firm will be able to compete against a big-box retailer on price, cutting costs on inventory provides the smaller firm with additional resources that can be used to invest in customer service and other forms of differentiation.

There are many other ways that small businesses partner with one another, from splitting the cost of a booth at a trade show to developing a joint advertising campaign. Many local businesses purchase their supplies and services from other local businesses rather than on the open market. This approach helps build camaraderie among locally owned firms and often encourages reciprocal buying and selling among locally owned companies. Big-box stores, which take their marching orders from corporate headquarters, are much less likely to engage in these types of activities.

Looking to Band Together with Other Local Businesses: Join or Start an Independent Business Alliance

An option that locally owned businesses have, that is becoming increasingly common across the country, is to form an *independent business alliance*. An independent business alliance is a nonprofit organization that is committed to nourishing and supporting locally owned firms. Examples include the Boulder Independent Business Alliance (Boulder, Colorado), the Austin Independent Business Alliance (Austin, Texas), and the Portland Independent Business & Community Alliance (Portland, Maine). A sample of the types of activities that independent business alliances perform follows:

- Sponsoring "buy local" campaigns
- Increasing public awareness of the positive economic benefits of shopping locally through feature articles, opinion editorials, local media coverage, and ongoing advocacy campaigns
- Providing locally owned businesses insignias that they can place in their store windows, on their menus or brochures, or in their advertising that designates them as a locally owned firm
- Facilitating networking events for locally owned business owners to get to know one another
- Printing and distributing directories of locally owned businesses

The networking events are particularly important and often lead to independent business owners forming partnerships, swapping business advice, and offering one another emotional support.

If you live in a community that doesn't have an independent business alliance and you're interested in starting one, you can obtain assistance from the American Independent Business Alliance (AMIBA) at www.amiba.net or the Business Alliance for Local Living Economics (BALLE) at www.livingeconomics.org.

Shop the Competition

A second tactic that new businesses utilize, particularly in the context of competing effectively against big-box retailers, is to shop the competition. The basic idea is that once a firm determines how it plans to compete against a larger rival, whether it is on product selection, product knowledge, or some other variable, it should continually assess whether it is maintaining the competitive edge it needs. In many instances, the only practical way to do this is to literally shop at the rival store.

Many business owners are transparent about how they go about this and will literally walk through a nearby Wal-Mart or Home Depot with a pad and pencil in hand. There are normally two objectives in mind when a person shops the competition. The first objective is to check on specific things like a competitor's product selection and prices. The second objective is to view the competitor's merchandise, get a sense of the general nature of the store, and get ideas that you might incorporate into your own store. There is nothing inherently unethical or improper about shopping at a rival's store as long as you are honest and are observing things that are in the open. There are also less intrusive ways to shop the competition, such as looking at its Web site and monitoring its print and media ads.

Business owners vary regarding how bold they are when shopping the competition. Sam Walton was known for frequently visiting Kmart and Target stores during the years he was building Wal-Mart and was reportedly often seen making notes in a spiral notebook or talking into a tape recorder while in a competitor's store.[12] It occasionally irks the manager of a store to see a competitor walking his or her aisle, knowing that comparison shopping is taking place. Some managers see comparison shopping as snooping and actually ask competitors to leave their stores. More often than not, however, it's a routine practice that doesn't raise any eyebrows.

One particular advantage of shopping the competition is that it allows you and your employees to speak more authoritatively to your own customers. Imagine the following scenario: You are the owner of an independent appliance store that sells big screen TVs, which is a product that is one of your biggest money makers. A customer comes into your store with an ad for a 56-inch plasma TV for $2,200 from a big-box store. You sell flat-panel LCD TVs (which use a different technology) and have a 56-inch model for $2,500. Your exchange with the customer might go like this:

Customer:

"How does your 56-inch LCD TV compare to the 56-inch plasma TV I can buy down the street? Your TV is $300 higher."

You:

"Our TV is better," you say without hesitation.

Customer:

"How do you know it's better? Have you seen the 56-inch plasma TV?"

You:

"No, I've never seen the 56-inch plasma TV, but I just know our LCD TV is better. Its brightness and sound quality are rated higher."

Customer:

"But you've never seen the difference with your own eyes? I don't want to pay $300 more for the LCD TV unless it's really better. It's hard for me to see a difference."

You:

"Sorry, I've never actually seen the 56-inch plasma TV."

Not very impressive is it? It would have been much better if you could have said that you've seen the 56-inch plasma TV and then talk about your impressions of the differences between the two TVs. In addition, if you had shopped the competition thoroughly, there would probably be other things you could talk about. For example, if you know you have a cost and convenience advantage over your competitor in regard to delivery and installation, you might say, "Another thing to keep in mind is that the store that carries the plasma TV charges $200 for delivery and installation. We only charge $100. We also deliver and install on weekends and holidays."

Summary

Many small businesses compete effectively against big-box stores, primarily by operating in niche markets and differentiating themselves from what the big-boxes have to offer. There is no denying that the big-box stores are formidable. Stores like Wal-Mart and Target serve hundreds of thousands of customers daily and are growing in stature. But small businesses have an important role to play in the marketplace, too. The most important thing for a new business to understand is how to position itself in a way that avoids direct competition with big-box retailers.

The next chapter focuses on the myth that it's almost impossible for a new business to get noticed. There are actually many ways for a new business to get noticed, but it takes some familiarity with the options and a willingness to persevere. Many business owners enjoy the process of spreading the word about the products or services they have to sell once they catch on to the most effective ways of going about it.

Endnotes

1   Gary McWilliams, "Wal-Mart Era Wanes Amid Big Shifts in Retail," *The Wall Street Journal*, October 3, 2007, A1.

2   Kenneth E. Stone, "Impact of the Wal-Mart Phenomenon on Rural Communities," in Proceedings of *Increasing Understanding of Public Problems and Policies*, 1997 (Chicago: Farm Foundation, 1998), Charts 5, 8, 9, and 11.

3   Andersonville Study home page, http://www.andersonvillestudy.com (accessed October 9, 2007).

4   Steve McLinden, "Who's Afraid of the Giant?" *Shopping Centers Today*, June 2006, http://www.schostak.com/table_pages/images/shop_ctrs_today_art.pdf (accessed October 2, 2007).

5   Edward Iwata, "Companies Can Grow In Goliaths' Shadows," *USA Today*, November 19, 2005.

6   Stone, "Impact of the Wal-Mart Phenomenon on Rural Communities."

7   Darrell K. Rigby and Dan Hass, "Outsmarting Wal-Mart," *Harvard Business Review* 12 (December 2004): 22, 26.

8   Gary McWilliams, "Wal-Mart Era Wanes Amid Big Shifts in Retail," *The Wall Street Journal*, October 3, 2007, A1.

9   B. Ruggiero, "Kazoo & Company Reaches Top 5...Again," *TD Monthly*, June 2005; J.M. Webb, "When the Tools of the Trade Are Toys," *TD Monthly*, March 2006.

10 Kelly L. Giraud, Craig A. Bond, and Jennifer J. Keeling, "Consumer Preferences for Locally Made Specialty Products Across Northern New England," (Department of Resource Economics and Development, University of New Hampshire, Durham, NH), 20.

11 Giraud, Bond, and Keeling, "Consumer Preferences for Locally Made Specialty Products Across Northern New England," 4.

12 Sam Walton and John Huey, *Sam Walton: Made In America* (New York: Doubleday, 1992).

CHAPTER 7

Myth No. 7:
It's Almost Impossible for a New Business to Get Noticed

Truth No. 7:
There Are Many Ways for New Businesses to Get Noticed and Recognized

Introduction

A deep-seated fear that many potential business owners have is that they will start their businesses, and no one will notice. Most of the time, the fear doesn't originate from a lack of confidence in the product or service the business will sell. Business owners normally go to great lengths to make sure their initial products or services are right. Instead, the fear originates from a lack of knowledge about how to make people aware of their businesses and how to market the products. The fear is heightened the first time a prospective business owner checks into the cost of print and media advertising. In a mid-sized city, a large newspaper ad can run as high as $15,000. That's more than the total start-up cost of many businesses! Another obstacle is the sheer tempo of ads in the marketplace. The average person is exposed to about 2,000 marketing messages a day.[1] It's no wonder that prospective business owners are fearful about their businesses not getting noticed.

Fortunately, there are inexpensive ways for businesses to get noticed and for their messages to reach their target markets. But there is a problem. The problem is that the majority of business owners are familiar with the most expensive ways to get a business noticed—print and media advertising—and are less familiar with more cost-efficient alternatives. As a result, many businesses struggle to get noticed because they can't afford to do a lot of advertising, and they either don't know about or don't take the time to pursue less expensive alternatives.

The truth is that it is possible for a new company to get noticed, but it takes three things to make it happen. First, it takes a business owner who is willing to learn about the full array of marketing-related techniques that are available. Second, it takes persistence and hard work. Many of the most cost-effective ways for a business to get noticed, from passing out brochures to writing a blog, are inexpensive, but they take time and effort. Third, it takes a focused and sensible marketing strategy.

To address these issues and further dispel the myth that it's almost impossible for a new business to get noticed, this chapter is divided into three sections. The first section provides three rules-of-thumb for approaching the challenge of getting noticed. It's important for a new business to approach this challenge carefully because an ill-advised approach to trying to get noticed can be costly and ineffective. The second section describes how a business establishes a brand. A brand is the set of attributes that people associate with a company. It's important for a business to think about its brand as part of its strategy for getting noticed because it wants to be thought of in a certain way. The third section describes the most common tactics and techniques that businesses use to get recognized or get noticed.

Rules-of-Thumb for How to Approach the Challenge of Getting Noticed

As discussed, increasing the visibility of a new business takes three things—familiarity with the alternatives, hard work, and a sensible strategy. Ironically, once you start investigating the various alternatives, the task becomes harder rather than easier. There are dozens of alternatives for marketing and promoting a business, from traditional print advertising, to attending trade shows, to posting a video on YouTube.com. There are also thousands of books and Web sites dedicated to marketing, advertising, public relations, and other forms of promotions. While these resources are helpful, the advice they provide is so plentiful and varied that it's hard for a new business owner to know where to start.

This section provides three rules-of-thumb for initiating the process of getting your business noticed.

Focus on a Niche Market and the Benefits Offered to Customers

The first rule-of-thumb is to focus singularly on your niche market and the benefits your business offers the targeted customers. While this advice sounds straightforward, not all businesses are clear regarding what their markets are and who they are trying to appeal to. As mentioned in previous chapters, a niche market is a place within a larger market segment that represents a narrow group of customers with similar needs. The reason it's important to know your niche market is that it's premature for a business to select, or even talk about, specific marketing techniques until it has a clear picture of who its customers will be. If a firm starts advertising or promoting its business before it's sure who its customers are, it will not only waste money but can confuse people who are unsure whether the product is intended for them.

It's also important for a business, as part of its initial efforts to get noticed, to draw attention to the factors that differentiate it from its competitors. This is a potentially make-it or break-it issue for many businesses. It's hard to get people to try something new or change their habits and behaviors and switch from a product they're currently using to a new one. As a result, you have to clearly explain how your a product is better or cheaper to get people to try it. It's typically best to limit the points you focus on to two or three points to make them memorable and distinct.

For example, ZUCA, the backpack on rollers introduced in Chapter 5, has two distinct points of differentiation: It relieves back pain by putting the backpack on rollers, and it is sturdy enough for either a child or an adult to sit on. At the time the ZUCA was introduced, these attributes were different enough from anything else on the market that the company got noticed, and its product took off.

Another activity that's important for a new business is to learn as much as it can about the people in its niche market, from how much disposable income they have to the periodicals they read and the Web sites they visit. This task can be completed by following prescriptions already discussed in this book. Laura Udall, the founder of ZUCA, conducted focus groups to learn about her target market.[2] She was also a mother, and her original insight for the ZUCA backpack came from watching her own daughter struggle with the backpacks she carried to school every day. Other methods, such as reading industry trade journals and surveying potential clients, are also good ideas.

The steps described here, which should precede your selection of specific tactics and techniques to get your business noticed, are shown in Figure 7.1.

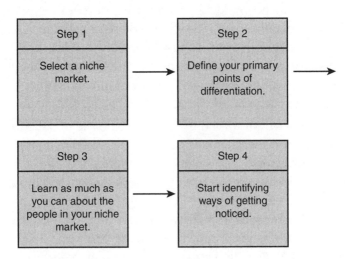

Figure 7.1 *Steps involved in initiating the process of getting a business noticed*

Selling Benefits Rather Than Features

In their attempts to gain visibility, many new businesses make the mistake of promoting the features rather than the benefits of their products or services. A promotional strategy that focuses on the features of a product, such as its technical merits, is almost always less effective than a strategy that focuses on the merits of what a product can *do* for the person buying it. For example, one of the most successful advertising campaigns ever launched by McDonald's contained ads that featured the jingle, "You deserve a break today—at McDonald's." McDonald's could have stressed the cleanliness of its stores or the uniformity of its french fries, both of which are features. Instead, it struck a chord with people by focusing on one of the biggest benefits of eating at McDonald's—not having to cook. Although not as obvious in today's society, not having to cook a meal at home was a major advantage when McDonald's started using this tagline.

The same rationale can be applied to any product or service. Consider the ZUCA rolling backpack. In her initial attempts to get the ZUCA noticed, Laura Udall could have talked about the ZUCA's durable aluminum frame, its oversized silent wheels, the washable nature of the bag, and the number of colors that were available. These are all features. It's much more likely that she focused on the benefits of the product—the fact that it relieves back pain and is durable enough that a child can sit on it while waiting for the school bus. (The ZUCA includes a fold out seat.) These are the benefits or the value that the ZUCA delivers to its users.

Consider Diverse Marketing Methods

The second rule-of-thumb pertaining to the challenge of getting a business noticed is to consider diverse marketing methods. The best approaches for learning about the methods that are available are to look through books and magazines on marketing and promotions and take a class from your local Small Business Development Center. Also, study companies that are selling products in the same market you will be targeting to see how they are gaining visibility and how they are marketing their products.

It is advisable to consider as many alternatives as possible before settling on the techniques you'll use to try to increase visibility. In some cases, the choices will be clear. For example, if you plan to launch a Web site to sell plus-sized clothing for children, the only way to reach your audience might be through pay-per-click Internet advertising (more about this option later). In other instances, the best choice or choices may be unclear, and it could take some guidance to find the best alternative. This scenario played out for Proactiv, the #1 seller of acne products in the United States, mentioned in Chapter 5. At one point early in the life of the company, it was suggested to Dr. Katie Rodan and Dr. Kathy Fields, the company's founders, that the best way to get the word out about Proactiv was via infomercials. Initially, the two were shocked because they had a low opinion of infomercials. But they got to thinking that an infomercial might be the best way to educate people about their products. Proactiv was revolutionary in that it was designed to prevent rather than simply treat acne. As a result, the product needed more explaining than could be accomplished in a 30-second television spot or a print ad. Acne is also an embarrassing problem, which made it unlikely that people would go into a store and ask for a detailed explanation of how Proactiv should be used. The following bulleted list lays out the points in favor of using infomercials to sell Proactiv.

- People need to be reeducated about how to treat acne.
- The reeducation can't be done in a 30-second or 60-second television commercial, or in a print ad.
- Acne is an embarrassing problem, so people will be most open to learning about it in the privacy of their homes.
- The demographic group that spends the most time watching infomercials, women in their 20s, 30s, and 40s, are Proactiv's market.
- Infomercials provide Proactiv the opportunity to show heartfelt testimonials of people who have used the

product. Showing "before" and "after" pictures of people who have used the product and have experienced dramatic results has been a particularly persuasive tactic.

Proactiv launched its first infomercial in 1994, and the vast majority of its customers have been introduced to its products through this medium. Ironically, Rodan and Fields would have never come up with the idea of using infomercials on their own. It took a suggestion from an outside party to alert the two founders to this possibility.[3]

An additional piece of advice that's provided to business owners when they're looking for ways to stand out is to think creatively and try new tactics and techniques. The rationale behind this advice is that a new business has to find a way to stand out. There are many examples of businesses that have followed this advice and have created original and fun ideas to draw attention to themselves. For example, to generate interest in Cranium, a board game for adults, the founder borrowed a trick learned from the makers of Trivial Pursuit. For $15,000, they recruited 100 radio stations around the country to have their DJs read Cranium questions over the air. The callers who phoned in the correct answers got a copy of the game as a prize (and everyone listening got introduced to the company). A similarly creative technique was utilized by Zach Nelson, the founder of MyCIO.com (now called McAfee ASaP), to get his business noticed:

> *"One of the great things we did when we first launched MyCIO.com is that we draped our entire eleven-story building on Highway 101 with the MyCIO.com logo. It was the world's largest billboard. The city of San Jose wasn't very happy with us for doing it, but they let us keep it up for a month. Everyone that I called after we ran that giant billboard I received a return call back from."*[4]

One pleasant surprise that many business owners experience when they start looking at the options for gaining visibility is that many of the alternatives are inexpensive. For example, 400,000 small businesses reportedly have blogs, which are inexpensive to create and maintain.[5] Similarly, it costs a business owner nothing to speak to a community group or to give an interview to a business magazine. These approaches can be effective ways to get the word out about a new company.

Find Ways to Build Credibility and Support

The third rule-of-thumb pertaining to the challenge of getting your business noticed is to build credibility and support for your company from the beginning. This is most effectively done by finding ways to get others to talk about or validate the merits of your business. While there is nothing inherently wrong with advertising and similar forms of promotion, people know that ads and promotions are paid for, so they discount them to a certain degree. It's normally much more persuasive when an unbiased third party talks about the merits of your product or service.

There are several ways to garner this type of support. Many businesses cultivate reference accounts. A reference account is an early user of a firm's product who is willing to give a testimonial regarding his or her experience with the product. To obtain reference accounts, new firms must often offer their products to a group of customers for free or at a reduced price in exchange for their willingness to try the product and for their feedback. There is nothing improper about this process as long as everything is kept aboveboard and the business is not indirectly "paying" someone to offer a positive endorsement. Once the testimonials are collected, they are used in company brochures, advertisements, and by salespeople who are able to tell potential customers about the positive experiences that other customers have had.

There are more formal ways to build credibility and support. Some businesses sell products that can be certified by an agency and can then place the agency's certification mark on their products. The most familiar certification mark is the UL mark, which certifies that a product meets the safety standards of Underwriters Laboratories. A similar example is the Good Housekeeping Seal of Approval. There are also industry-specific seals of authenticity or approval. An example is the "100 Percent Napa Valley" certification mark, which can only go on bottles of wine where 100% of the grapes used to produce the wine were grown in the Napa Valley of Northern California. If similar certifications are available for the product or service your business plans to offer, it is well worth your time to try to obtain the certification.

There are also occasions when a business benefits when a core aspect of what it's doing meets a standard that is viewed favorably by the pubic. An example of this is provided by White Wave, a company that makes soy milk. In 1996, White Wave came up with a new idea for selling soymilk. It would produce a dry soy mixture, ship it to dairies, pay the dairies to add water, package the resulting soymilk in milk-like containers, and distribute the product. Initially, the going was slow. Then the company caught a big break. In October 1999, the FDA announced that soy was considered a heart-healthy substance that could lower cholesterol. This announcement provided the legitimacy White Wave needed to take its soymilk mainstream, which was its goal from the beginning. White Wave Silk Soymilk is now found in the dairy section of almost every grocery store in the United States.[6]

One additional way businesses build credibility and support, which is talked about in more depth later, is by having favorable articles written about them in newspapers, magazines, and trade journals.[7] It also helps a business to win an award.

For example, in 2007 White Wave's Silk Soymilk won the American Culinary ChefsBest Award for Best Taste. White Wave can now refer to the award in its advertising and has earned the right to display the ChefsBest seal of approval on its products.[8]

Establishing a Brand

A brand is a set of attributes—positive or negative—that people associate with a business. These attributes can be positive, such as trustworthy, innovative, dependable, or easy to deal with, or they can be negative, such as poor-quality, unreliable, sloppy, or difficult to deal with. In our experience, it's important that a new business give thought to the brand it plans to develop before it initiates any marketing or promotional activities. The first impression that a business makes with its potential customers should convey the essence of how it wants to be viewed and seen.

New businesses must build a brand from scratch, which starts with selecting the company's name. One of the keys to effective branding is to create a strong personality for a firm, designed to appeal to its target market. Southwest Airlines, for example, has created a brand that denotes fun. This is a good fit for its target market: people traveling for pleasure rather than business. Similarly, Starbucks has created a brand that denotes an experience framed around warmth and hospitality, encouraging people to linger and buy additional products. A business ultimately wants its customers to strongly identify with it—to see themselves as "Southwest Airlines flyers" or "Starbucks coffee drinkers." People won't do this, however, unless they see a business as being different from its competitors in ways that create a special and valuable experience for them.

The First Step in a Company's Branding Strategy: Selecting Its Name

While at first glance naming a business might seem like a minor issue, it is an extremely important one. A company's name is one of the first things people associate with a business, and it is a word or phrase that will be said thousands or hundreds of thousands of times during the life of a business. A company's name is also the most critical aspect of its branding strategy. It's important that a business's name facilitate rather than hinder how the business wants to differentiate itself in the marketplace and how it wants to be viewed by its customers.

A useful way to discuss this issue is to divide companies into four categories:

Consumer-Driven Companies

If a company plans to focus on a particular type of customer, its name should reflect the attributes of its clientele. For example, a high-end clothing store that specializes in small sizes for women is called La Petite Femme. Similarly, a company introduced in Chapter 1, Type 1 and Type 2 Tools, helps children with diabetes cope with their disease. These names were chosen to appeal specifically to their target markets or clientele.

Product- or Service-Driven Companies

If a company plans to focus on a particular product or service, its name should reflect the advantages that its product or service brings to the marketplace. Examples include Jiffy Print, ServiceMaster, Daisy Rock Guitars, and 1-800-CONTACTS. These names were chosen to reflect the distinctive attributes of the product or service the company offers, regardless of the clientele.

Industry-Driven Companies

If a company plans to focus on a broad range of product or services in a particular industry, its name should reflect the category it is participating in. Examples include General Motors, Bed Bath & Beyond, and Home Depot. These companies have names that are intentionally broad and are not limiting in regard to target market or product selection.

Personality- or Image-Driven Companies

Some companies are founded by individuals who put such as indelible stamp on the company that it might be smart to name the company after the founder. Examples include DarynKagan.com, Charles Schwab, The Trump Organization, and Magic Johnson Enterprises. These companies have names that benefit from a positive association with a particular person or distinctive founder. Of course, this strategy can backfire if the founder falls out of favor in the public's eye.

So how does a new business develop a brand? On a philosophical level, a business must have meaning in its customers' lives. It must create value—something for which customers are willing to pay. Imagine a father shopping for airline tickets so that he can take his two children to see their grandparents for Christmas. If Southwest Airlines can get his family to their destination for $75 per ticket cheaper than its competitors, Southwest has real meaning in the father's life. Similarly, if a young couple buys a Cranium board game, and playing the game with other couples results in lasting friendships, then Cranium will have a special place in their hearts. Firms that create meaning in their customers' lives stand for something in terms of benefits, whether it is low prices, fun, fashion, quality, friendliness, improved health, or something else. This means creating a bond between a company and its customers.

On a more practical level, brands are built through the techniques we talked about in the third section of this chapter, which include advertising, public relations, media interviews, and other techniques. A firm's name, logo, Web site design, and even its letterhead are part of its brand. The most powerful metaphor that can be used to describe a brand is that it's a promise that a business makes to its customers. Other ways of thinking about the meaning of a brand are included in the following bulleted list.[9]

- A brand is a promise.
- A brand is a guarantee.
- A brand is a pledge.
- A brand is a reputation.
- A brand is an unwritten warrantee.
- A brand is an expectation of performance.
- A brand is a presentation of credentials.
- A brand is a mark of trust and reduced risk.
- A brand is a collection of memories.
- A brand is a handshake between a company and its customers.

The Most Common Tactics and Techniques for Getting a New Business Noticed

There are a number of tactics and techniques available to business owners to get their businesses noticed. Because most businesses are started with limited funds, as many alternatives as possible should be considered. In the majority of cases, a business will use a combination of techniques rather than rely on one or two. Serendipity and luck also play a role. Once the word gets out about a new product, like the ZUCA rolling backpack, the company is often contacted and asked for interviews and similar opportunities. It is normally to a business owner's advantage to pursue as many of these opportunities as possible, as long as the end-result positively reflects on the business and its brand.

This section discusses the most commonly used techniques for getting a business noticed. The section is divided into four categories: advertising, public relations, Internet-related methods (other than pay-per-click advertising), and word-of-mouth marketing.

Want to Save Time When an Advertising Salesperson Calls on You? Use These Three Criteria

One thing that happens to new businesses is that they are generally inundated by other businesses that want to sell them advertising or some other form of promotion. The challenge for a new business is to sort out the possibilities that make sense from those that don't. There are three criteria that a business can use to quickly make decisions in this area, and utilizing them can help save time and heartache in dealing with advertising salespeople.

Criterion #1: Will my target market see the ad? The first question to consider is whether your target market will even see the proposed ad. For example, if your target market is teenage boys, it's unlikely that they'd see an ad

in a local classified magazine—the type that is distributed at grocery stores and gas stations. Because
teenagers spend so much time online, a better choice
might be placing an ad on Craigslist or a similar Web
site. As a side benefit, advertising on Craigslist is usually free.

Criterion #2: Is the ad or promotion consistent with my
brand? Certain types of ads and promotions will be consistent with your brand, and others won't. For example,
if you're opening a sporting goods store, buying bill-
board space at a local high school football stadium
might be fully appropriate. It would be silly for someone
with an upscale clothing boutique to pursue the same
type of promotion—it just doesn't fit.

Criterion #3: Is the ad or promotion within my budget?
Be leery of expensive advertising and promotions alternatives. Stay within a reasonable budget. There are so
many inexpensive alternatives available that you should
exhaust your investigation of these options before you
spend a lot of money.

Advertising

There are many different ways that businesses advertise. While
it's normally cost-prohibitive for a new business to advertise on
television and in major newspapers and magazines, there are
other alternatives that are less expensive or free. The two major
categories of advertising include print and media advertising
and Internet advertising. The following is a discussion of each
category with an emphasis on the alternatives most suitable for
new businesses.

Print and Media Advertising

Print and media advertising runs the gamut from television ads
to posting flyers on grocery store bulletin boards. The type of
advertising a firm selects hinges largely on whether it is targeting

a national audience, like an e-commerce site that plans to sell hunting and fishing gear, or a local clientele, like a single-store woman's clothing boutique. There are some advertising-related initiatives that all new businesses should take advantage of. For example, the major Internet search engines, like Google and Yahoo!, have business directories that list local businesses and in some cases even provide a map to show where they are located. You can get your business listed but have to go to the Web sites and sign up. The listings are either free or are subject to a small yearly charge. If you want to see how this works, type "hardware stores in Wichita, Kansas" into the Google search engine and see what happens. The names of the "local businesses" that appear have registered their businesses in the Google business directory.

New businesses that plan to target a local clientele typically avoid television, newspaper, and magazine advertising because of the costs involved. As mentioned earlier, a large ad in the newspaper of a mid-sized city can cost as much as $15,000. Radio advertising is effective for many businesses that have a local station with a listening audience that reflects the demographic they're trying to reach. Classified ads, either in local newspapers or online, remain effective in many instances. Direct mail, placing an ad in a local business directory, and advertising in publications such as local homeowners' association newsletters are additional choices. A business's own signage and visibility can be its most important form of advertising. Some home remodeling businesses, for example, report that their #1 source for getting new business is people who see their trucks parked in neighborhoods and call the phone number displayed on the sides of the trucks.

Television, newspaper, and mainstream magazine advertising is also avoided by businesses that plan to target a national clientele. The challenges these businesses have is how to reach their specific niche market. There are several ways to do this. There are literally thousands of magazines that target narrow niches. In some cases, a magazine might even help finance a company's initial ads if it thinks the company looks promising and could become a regular advertiser. Another option is to advertise in industry trade journals, if that's a good fit. A trade journal is a periodical, magazine, or publication that focuses on a specific industry, trade, or type of business. A directory of trade associations (which publish trade journals) is available through Weddle's at www.weddles.com/associations/index.cfm. Many trade associations also sponsor trade shows and conferences where new businesses can gain visibility and display their products.

Internet Advertising

An increasingly effective way for all new businesses to get noticed and sell their products is via pay-per-click Internet advertising. This type of advertising is provided by the major search engines, such as Google, Yahoo!, and MSN. Google has two pay-per-click programs—AdWords and AdSense. AdWords allows an advertiser to buy keywords on Google's home page, which triggers text-based ads to the side (and sometimes above) the search results when the keyword is used. So if you type "fishing equipment" into the Google search bar, you will see ads from Bass Pro Shop, Cabela's, and other companies that have fishing equipment to sell. Many businesses report impressive results utilizing this approach, presumably because they are able to place their ads in front of people who are already searching for information about their products. Google's other pay-per-click program is called AdSense. It is similar to AdWords, except the advertiser's ads appear on other Web sites instead of Google's home page. A full explanation of how AdSense works is provided in Chapter 8.

There are businesses that have relied almost exclusively on pay-per-click advertising to get noticed and to sell their products. These businesses often sell a product that wouldn't sell in sufficient volume to support a brick-and-mortar store. For example, Oddball Shoe Company (www.oddballshoe.com), an online shoe store, sells a size 16 EEEE athletic shoe for men and similar odd sized shoes. People find out about Oddball Shoe when they search for unusual sized shoes on Google and see the company's ad alongside their search results. Pay-per-click advertising has also allowed some people to turn their hobbies into businesses. For example, a Web site named SeatGuru (www.seatguru.com) was started by a flying enthusiast and lists the best seats and the worst seats (in terms of comfort) for each airline by type of aircraft. Prior to the advent of the Google AdSense program, the site had no practical way of making money. Now the site is viable as a for-profit business as a result of participating in the Google AdSense program. If you look at the site, you'll see a number of targeted ads sponsored by the Google AdSense program.

Public Relations

One of the most cost-effective ways for a new business to get noticed and to continually promote its products is through public relations. Public relations refers to efforts to establish and maintain a company's brand and the image associated with the brand to the public. The major difference between public relations and advertising is that public relations is not paid for—directly. The cost of public relations to a business is the effort it takes to network with journalists and other people to try to interest them in saying or writing good things about a company and its products. Examples of public relations techniques include:

- Press releases
- Media coverage
- Articles about the business in local newspapers, national magazines, or industry press
- Monthly newsletter
- Sponsor free seminars
- Contribute expert "how-to" or advice articles in your local newspaper
- Civic, social, and community involvement

In most cases, public relations is better than advertising because it is more grass roots and isn't seen as self-serving as advertising. The key to getting good public relations, such as a newspaper or magazine article written about your company, is to create a human-interest story that's associated with your firm. It also helps to be proactive in regard to speaking out on behalf of your industry and talking to trade groups and civic groups about your industry or area of expertise.

An example of how these efforts come together to create positive public relations and help a business get noticed is provided by Lisa Druxman, the founder of Stroller Strides (www.stroller-strides.com), a franchise organization for new mothers. Stroller Strides is a concept that Druxman developed to get herself back in shape after her first baby was born. It is an organized workout class where women push strollers, power-walk, and exercise outdoors to meet their fitness goals and socialize with other mothers. Prior to starting Stroller Strides, Druxman was the general manager of a health club. Druxman's story is a classic illustration of how public relations works and the potential payoffs involved:

> *"When I (was) the general manager at the health club, I would regularly go on the news promoting new workouts. One day the TV station called me and asked, 'Would you mind coming in with your baby and give (some) tips on how to get back in shape?' So I did, and I promoted my class as if it were this big business—I gave out my home e-mail and personal cell phone number. By the time I got home from the station, I had 75 calls and emails from all over San Diego from people who were interested in taking my class. I had my grand opening class three weeks after that, with 40 people there and more news coverage."*[10]

The key to Druxman's success, in this instance, was that she was able to tell her story through an unbiased third party, the TV program. Her story was compelling enough that it drew more free publicity in the form of news coverage of her grand opening. Many startups seek similar types of public relations through stories in local newspapers or business journals or through a national publication like *Fortune Small Business* or *Entrepreneur*. The key to getting this type of coverage is to have an interesting story to tell rather than simply extolling the value of your product or service.

There are many other ways in which a new business can enhance its chances of getting recognized by the press. One technique is to prepare a press kit, which is a folder that contains background information about the company and includes a list of its most recent accomplishments. The kit is normally distributed to journalists and is placed on the business's Web site. In fact, if you've ever picked up a national magazine and read an article about a business in a small town and wondered how the magazine knew about the business, it's typically because the business sent the magazine a press kit and the business's story (or product or service) fit the article the magazine was interested in writing. Another technique is to attend industry trade shows. Members of the media often attend trade shows to get the latest industry news. For example, the largest trade show for consumer electronics is International CES, which is held in Las Vegas every January. Many new technology firms use this show to present their products to the public for the first time. They do this in part because they have a captive media audience that is eager to find interesting stories to write about.

Internet-Related Methods
(Other Than Pay-Per-Click Advertising)

Business owners are increasing utilizing the Internet as a medium for increasing their visibility. Two techniques, other than pay-per-click advertising, are blogging and social networking.

BLOGGING

As mentioned earlier, approximately 400,000 businesses now maintain blogs. A blog is a Web site where entries are written in chronological order (similar to a diary). A typical blog contains text entries, images, links to other blogs, and space for readers to leave comments in an interactive format.

The idea behind blogs, in regard to helping a business get noticed, is they familiarize people with a business and help build an emotional bond between a business and its customers. An example is a blog written by Mary Baker, the co-owner of Dover Canyon Winery (http://dovercanyon.typepad.com/dover_canyon). Baker started her blog in April, 2006, using a software package called TypePad Pro that costs her $149.50 a year to maintain. She uses the blog to give her readers periodic updates on what's happening at the winery and how she feels about her life and her business. She also posts pictures of herself, her pets, her family, and daily life at the winery. To make her customers aware of the blog, she drops a postcard with the blog's address into bags with customer purchases. There is also a link to the blog on Dover Canyon Winery's Web site. Mail-order sales for the winery almost doubled from 2006 to 2007.[11]

An example of a business owner who credits his blog for the success of his business is Steve Spangler, the owner of Steve Spangler Science. Spangler's Web site sells science kits and experiments for children and adults. In his blog, titled Steve Spangler's Secrets (www.stevespangler.com), he talks about science and describes experiments that can be done safely with common everyday household items. Spangler gained national attention after a video of him demonstrating the explosive effects of dropping Mentos into two liter bottles of soda spread across the Internet. If you haven't seen the video, it is really fun. Just go to YouTube.com and type in "the original mentos geyser video." The spread of the video and the recognition it has brought him sold Spangler on the value of the Internet for getting the word out about a company. Steve Spangler Science is reportedly generating more than $5 million in annual sales.[12]

SOCIAL NETWORKING

Social Networking Web sites are ones that bring together people with common interests to share those interests and interact with one another. Most sites provide a variety of ways for users to interact and get to know one another including chat, messaging, e-mail, video, voice chat, file sharing, and discussion groups. Users are generally permitted to build their own profile pages where they can post information about themselves. Most social networking sites are free and have a directory that makes it easy for a user to zero-in on a specific area of interest.

An example of a social networking site is CraftBuddy.com, a site specifically designed for people who make, enjoy, and sell crafts. On the site, users can easily identify crafters with similar interests, view their profiles to learn more about them, and look at photos of their crafts. As a result, it's a good place for anyone starting a craft or craft-related business to showcase his or her company and get feedback on products. Social networking sites vary in terms of whether they allow advertising and e-commerce to take place. Some sites do not allow their users to advertise, overtly promote their products, or conduct e-commerce on their sites. Others sites, like CraftBuddy.com, have a business directory where members can post links to their commercial Web sites.

There are also more broad-based social networking sites like MySpace.com and Facebook (www.facebook.com). These sites are multifunctional platforms that allow their users to collect friends, build professional networks, and create or join groups of similarly minded people. MySpace has approximately 200 million users worldwide. While MySpace is technically intended for noncommercial use, many businesses post pictures of their products and subtly advertise on their MySpace profiles. MySpace has a feature called "Bulletin" that allows you to post messages which are broadcast to every person on your friends list. You can also set up a blog. Many people that write about MySpace warn against building a large network of friends and then spamming them with subtle advertisements and product promotions. Starbuck's MySpace profile is an example of a well-done business profile. You can view it by going to MySpace.com and typing Starbucks in the search engine. Creating a Facebook profile is similar to MySpace and provides many of the same advantages.

The key to determining whether it's worth your effort to set up a MySpace or Facebook profile is whether you think people in your niche market would find you on the site and participate in your network.

Word-of-Mouth Marketing

The fourth category of techniques that business owners use to get their businesses noticed is word-of-mouth marketing. This technique, which is also called buzz or viral marketing, involves getting people to spread the word about a new product or service via face-to-face conversations, e-mail, text messaging, or through other means. Word-of-mouth marketing is effective in part because people are more inclined to follow-up on a product recommendation from a friend or acquaintance than a paid advertisement.

Most word-of-mouth campaigns are initiated through some form of "seeding" in which key individuals or groups of individuals are utilized to get the initiative going. Seeding typically involves giving away samples of products or allowing people to preview a product before it is available to the general public. It also involves steps that reinforce or encourage the word-of-mouth once it's started.

An example of a successful word-of-mouth campaign is provided by PowerBar, the first energy bar on the market. PowerBar's founder, Brian Maxwell, couldn't afford to advertise his product, so he launched what he referred to as a "grass roots seeding" effort to get the company noticed. The first thing Maxwell did, with the help of his girlfriend (and later wife) Jennifer Biddulph, was to go to every sporting event in the San Francisco area (which is where they lived) and talk to people about the product. Between the two of them, they spoke to over 1,200 people. Once the product was ready, Maxwell sent the people they talked to a little box containing five PowerBars and a follow-up survey. This got people talking about PowerBar and sharing the product with their friends. The next move is legendary. To stimulate word-of-mouth in other areas of the country, Maxwell sent a letter to his existing customers offering to send five PowerBars on their behalf to anyone in the United States for just a $3.00 shipping fee. He even put a note in every box that said "To Brian from Sarah in San Francisco" (or whatever the applicable names were). This effort jump-started word-of-mouth about PowerBar in different parts of the country.

As the word-of-mouth surrounding PowerBar grew, Maxwell turned his focus to "seeding" various sports. He identified influential people in each sport and hired them to be PowerBar spokespersons and gave them a certain number of PowerBars to give away. This effort stimulated word-of-mouth surrounding PowerBar in multiple sports. At one point early in the life of

PowerBar, Maxwell was approached by the captain of the U.S. Cycling Team that was preparing to represent the United States in the Tour de France. The person asked Maxwell to donate 1,000 PowerBars to the team. Maxwell hesitated but agreed. On a Saturday, three weeks later, right in the middle of the Tour de France, CBS, which was covering the event, did a three-minute segment on PowerBar, a new "energy bar" the U.S. team was eating. Maxwell couldn't believe his good fortune. That single broadcast created word-of-mouth discussions about PowerBar in thousands of different places.[13]

While not all word-of-mouth campaigns will contain the same elements as the PowerBar campaign, the gist of what Maxwell did is reflective of successful word-of-mouth campaigns. He "seeded" initial users of his product and then created incentives to encourage them to talk up the product among their friends and acquaintances.

Summary

This chapter illustrates the importance of being familiar with the start-up process. A simple awareness of the most cost-effective ways to getting noticed and how to go about implementing them can save a business owner a substantial amount of money and produce better results in the long run. It's simply no longer necessary for a new business to rely strictly on print and media advertising to gain visibility. Many of the methods discussed in this chapter, some of which are virtually free, are equally effective in increasing the visibility and legitimacy of a new business.

The next chapter focuses on the myth that the Internet isn't all it was hyped up to be. Actually, we think you'll come away from reading the chapter with just the opposite impression— that the Internet is a marvelous tool. In the chapter, we discuss the factors that facilitate Internet business success along with the most common ways that businesses and individuals make money online.

Endnotes

1 Shel Horowitz, *Grassroots Marketing: Getting Noticed in a Noisy World* (New York: Chelsea Green, 2000).

2 ZUCA home page, http://www.zuca.com (accessed October 15, 2007).

3 Proactiv home page, http://www.proactiv.com (accessed October 15, 2007); K. Rodan, "Entrepreneurial Thought Leaders."

4 M.W. Ragas, *Lessons From the eFront* (New York: Prima Publishing, 2001), 181.

5 Rachael King, "Make Some Noise," *BusinessWeek SmallBiz*, August/September 2007, 71.

6 Emanuel Rosen, *The Anatomy of Buzz* (New York: Doubleday, 2000).

7 Al Ries and Laura Ries, *The Fall of Advertising and the Rise of PR* (New York: HarperCollins, 2002).

8 Silk Soymilk home page, http://www.silksoymild.com (accessed October 18, 2007).

9 Source: Adapted from D. Travis, *Emotional Branding: How Successful Brands Gain the Irrational Edge* (Roseville, CA: Prima Ventures, 2000).

10 Ladies Who Launch, accessed June 27, 2007 (see chap. 1, n. 4).

11 "Tram the Grapes, Write the Blog," *BusinessWeek SmallBiz*, August/September 2007, 72.

12 Business-Opportunities home page, http://www.husiness-opportunities.biz, (accessed October 15, 2007).

13 J.F. Kelly, *The Breakaway Brand* (New York: McGraw-Hill, 2005); Rosen, *The Anatomy of Buzz.*

Myth No. 8:
The Internet Isn't What It Was All Hyped Up to Be

Truth No. 8:
There Are Many Legitimate and Enjoyable Ways to Make Money Online

Introduction

An unfortunate myth that discourages people who otherwise could make a good living as business owners is the belief that the Internet isn't all it was hyped up to be. It's not difficult to understand where this sentiment comes from. During the Internet bubble, which lasted from 1995 to early 2001, there were predictions that the Internet would change everything and that brick-and-mortar stores were doomed. After the bubble burst, and thousands of Internet companies went out of business, it became clear that there had been some over-exuberance involved. It's hard to forget the spectacle of companies like Pets.com, with its playful sock puppet, losing its investors' millions of dollars and the sharp decline in the stock market. One Internet stock, Yahoo!, declined from $118.75 a share on January 3, 2000, to $4.06 on September 26, 2001.

Fortunately, the stock market recovered, and the Internet has proven to be resilient.

In fact, the number of Internet users worldwide has almost tripled since early 2001.[1] The number of businesses, shoppers, and people making a living online is also sharply up. It is estimated that United States online sales will increase 17.5% a year from 2007 until 2011.[2] Other activities online are also growing. For example, as mentioned in Chapter 7, approximately 400,000 businesses now maintain blogs, up from near zero in 2004 when business people started blogging.[3]

The truth is that the Internet has turned out to be a remarkable tool and platform. There are a growing number of ways that individuals and businesses are making money online. In fact, one of the beauties of the Internet is that people don't necessarily have to have products or services to sell to make money.

If someone knows a great deal about a particular topic, such as cooking or home repair, she can launch a Web site, populate it with articles, tips, and other useful information and make money online by essentially selling access to the people she attracts to her Web site. This is done primarily by selling advertising space on the Web site, as will be discussed throughout the chapter, to companies who sell products or services of interest to the visitors to the site. This one factor alone has enabled numerous people to convert hobbies and personal interests into part-time and full-time businesses.

To more fully discuss these topics and further dispel the myth that the Internet isn't all it was hyped up to be, this chapter proceeds in the following manner. First, we describe three factors that facilitate Internet-related business success. Second, we describe the most common ways that individuals and businesses make money online. Third, we describe the manner in which the Internet provides a platform for the sale of products and services produced by people working on a freelance basis.

Factors That Facilitate Internet-Related Business Success

Of the many factors contributing to Internet-related business success, three stand out—acquiring Internet-related knowledge and expertise, attracting users, and patience. Many people are not successful making money online primarily because they fall short on one or more of these important factors. Let's learn more about each factor.

Acquiring Internet-Related Knowledge and Expertise

The first factor that contributes to Internet-related success is acquiring Internet-related knowledge and expertise. While you don't have to be a computer geek to launch and run a successful Web site or other Internet application, you do need a certain level of expertise. For example, even if you hire someone to build your Web site or blog, you will normally maintain it and update it yourself. If you decide to monetize the site by participating in an affiliate or pay-per-click program, you'll need to know how to set these programs up. For example, if a business is approved by Google to display AdSense ads, you'll be provided some JavaScript code to paste into the html document that underlies your Web site. While this task isn't difficult you have to know what you're doing. In addition, the more you know about html (the main language for Web sites) and Web site design, the better you'll be at moving the ads around your site to see where they perform the best.

It's also important to know the basics of how the Internet works, particularly as it relates to how to obtain an Internet domain name, how to find a company to host your Web site, how to set up an e-mail account that corresponds to your Internet address, and so on. It's also helpful to know as much as possible about your options before you settle on how to utilize the Internet. For example, if you make crafts at home and plan to sell them online, you might not need your own Web site. You could sell them on eBay or another auction Web site. You could also utilize a service like Etsy (www.etsy.com), which is an online marketplace for the buying and selling of handmade products. If you become an Etsy member, the company will set up an online storefront for you.

The best way to get up-to-speed on these and similar topics is to read Internet-related books and magazines and find help through other reliable sources. Small Business Development

Centers often host seminars and workshops on how to start an Internet business. There are also companies that specialize in helping people design Web sites and set up Internet businesses. While many of these companies are legitimate, be careful. There are companies that prey on people who hope to "get rich quick" on the Internet and insist on being paid upfront. Make sure to check out any company before doing any business with them and ask for the names and phone numbers of people who they've helped before. If they won't provide names and phone numbers, look elsewhere.

Attracting Users

Regardless of the type of Internet business you start, one of your main goals will be to attract users or visitors to your site. A large measure of a Web site or blog's value is the total number of unique visitors it attracts on a weekly or monthly basis and the match between the demographic makeup of the visitors (that is, gender, age, occupation, interests, and income level) and the product or topic the site is promoting. The money a Web site or blog can generate is also roughly proportional to the amount of traffic it can produce.

As a result of these realities, it's important to take steps to attract people to your Web site or blog and to increase your traffic over time. There are several ways to do this. It's important to launch a site that satisfies its visitors. This means good quality products and services and a pleasant shopping experience for e-commerce sites, and rich content for blogs and special interest Web sites. These positive attributes keep people coming back and engender word-of-mouth referrals. The degree to which the people who launch a Web site or blog are passionate about their businesses also shows. It takes a lot of work to launch a well-designed, fully functional, and content-rich Web site or blog. If you throw something up quickly primarily to try to make money, it normally won't fly.

There are also specific steps that can be taken to drive traffic to your Web site. One step is to become an expert in your field and write articles and columns and frequently post comments on the blogs of others. Work should always be signed, and the business's Web site address should be listed. When you do this, you are giving people who have an interest in what you have to sell a way to "reach you" through your Web site.

There are also online article directories, such as Free Article Depot (http://free-article-depot.com), which people contribute to for free, hoping that a Web site will pick up the article and post it on its site. These articles have a signature box at the end, which provides you space to tell the reader about yourself, list key-words that pertain to the article, and provide your Web site address. Doing this directs people to your Web site, which is then picked up by the major search engines. As a result, the more articles posted, and the more Web sites that publish them, the earlier your business will appear in Google and Yahoo! search results. Some people claim that the best articles they've posted on Free Article Depot or Ezine Article (another directory) have spread to over 10,000 Web sites within a week. The key is to write articles that Web site owners see as valuable or interesting.

There is also an entire science referred to as Search Engine Optimization (SEO), which suggests additional techniques to get a business's name moved up in search engine results. The idea is that the earlier your business's name appears in search engine listings, the more people will click the link and visit your site. There are many resources, including books, magazine articles, and Web sites, that provide information on this topic.

Patience

Patience is a third factor that contributes to Internet-related success. It takes time and effort to successfully launch an Internet business and build traffic. Because of this, many Internet companies start as part-time businesses, adding content and visitors over time, before they're able to make much money. Top-tier companies only advertise on Web sites and blogs once they've reached a certain threshold of traffic. As a result, if you started a blog that focused on running marathons, you might need to post entries on your blog two or three times a week, write articles to draw attention to your blog, and promote your blog in other ways for several months or longer before you have enough traffic to attract good quality advertisers. People who don't understand this can become easily frustrated. Unless you have a generous advertising budget to promote your site, it will take time for users to find you regardless of how good you are.

It also takes patience and restraint, after you launch your Web site or blog, to resist the temptation to try to do too much too fast. As just mentioned, the primary way to build a successful Internet business is to satisfy users. For e-commerce sites, this means targeting a specialized niche market first rather than trying to tackle broad markets. In the case of a specialty Web site or blog, it means adding advertising slowly rather than quickly to avoid irritating early users. The cardinal rule in building an Internet business is to focus on quality first, and the money will follow.

The Most Common Ways That Individuals and Businesses Make Money Online

There are a growing number of ways that individuals and businesses are making money online. In fact, when the dot-com bubble burst in early 2001, most of the money-making tactics and techniques described here didn't exist. The Internet is a much healthier marketplace today, with multiple legitimate ways for individuals and businesses to sell products and services online and to monetize other types of Internet applications.

The following is a discussion of the six most common ways individuals and businesses make money online. An overview of the most familiar ways the Internet is used, along with an identification of money-making techniques that are most commonly utilized in those areas, is included in Table 8.1.

Table 8.1 How Businesses Make Money with Internet-Related Activities

Internet-Related Activities	Money-Making Techniques	Representative Businesses
E-commerce Web site	Direct sales, subscription fees, commissions	Amazon.com, SmugMug, Redfin

Internet-Related Activities	Money-Making Techniques	Representative Businesses
Business Web site (that supports a primarily off-line business)	Direct sales	Screenlife, Real Cosmetics, Yogitoes
Informative Special Interest Web site (often operated by hobbyists and enthusiasts)	AdSense, affiliate programs, direct sales, subscription fees	Zillow.com, SeatGuru.com, Askthebuilder.com
Social networking Web site	AdSense, affiliate programs, subscription fees	Facebook, Dogster.com, Quentin's Friends
Blog	Adsense, affiliate programs, direct sales	JoelComm.com, TechCrunch, TheMommyBlog
Auction Web site	Commissions, AdSense	eBay, StubHub, uBid.com

Affiliate Programs

An *affiliate program* is a way for online merchants, like 1-800-Flowers or Amazon.com, to get more exposure by offering a commission to Web sites and blogs that are willing to feature ads for their products or services. In most cases, the ads are small text ads, and the merchant sponsoring the program pays the affiliate a small commission every time someone clicks the ads and buys one of its products or services. eBay and similar membership sites have a slightly different type of program. If you're an eBay affiliate, you get paid $25 to $35 every time someone clicks the eBay ad on your site, creates an eBay account, and places a bid within 30 days. You also get between 50% and 75% of eBay's revenue on all winning bids or Buy It Nows (BINs) within seven days of the click.[4] Some online merchants have extensive affiliate programs. 1-800-Flowers, for example, has more than 40,000 affiliates.

The beauty of participating in an affiliate program, from the perspective of the owner of a Web site or a blog, is that you can make money on your site without incurring the costs involved with creating your own product or service and providing customer support. Your job is to attract people to your Web site or blog, and every time they click on your affiliate marketer's link, you get paid. This approach allows people who are experts in certain areas, like fitness, health care, or investments, to put up Web sites and seemingly give away vast amounts of information. The way they typically make money is by participating in affiliate programs and/or pay-per-click programs, which are described next.

There are two ways to get involved in affiliate programs. Many online merchants place information about how to sign up for their affiliate programs on their Web sites. For example, on Overstock.com, toward the bottom of its home page, there is a link that reads "Become an Affiliate." This link describes Overstock.com's affiliate program, including the commission rate they're currently paying. At the time this book was written, Overstock.com was offering an 8% commission. That means that if you created a Web site and became an Overstock.com affiliate, every time someone clicked through to Overstock.com's Web site from your Web site and spent $1,000, you'd get paid $80. Some affiliate programs are even more lucrative. Amazon.com has offered up to a 20% commission on MP3 downloads that originate through one of its affiliate's sites.

You can also work through a company that manages affiliate programs for others. Examples of companies that do this are Commission Junction (www.cj.com), Link Share (www.linkshare.com), and ShareASale (www.shareasale.com). These companies have access to thousands of online merchants that have affiliate programs. Their job is to find the best match between firms that sponsor affiliate programs and the Web sites and blogs that have the most potential to generate click-throughs to their sites.

Pay-Per-Click Programs

The second way that individuals and businesses make money online is through pay-per-click programs. The basic idea behind these programs is similar to an affiliate program. A Web site or blog allows an advertiser's link to be placed on its site and gets paid a small commission every time someone clicks the ad.

All of the major search engines sponsor pay-per-click programs. Examples include Google AdSense, Yahoo! Search Marketing, and MSN Adcenter. Google's AdSense program is by far the best-known and the largest. You've seen AdSense ads many times as you've looked at Web sites and blogs. They are easy to spot because they have a small emblem underneath the ads that says "Ads by Google."

Anyone with a Web site, blog, or other Internet application that has content can apply to participate in a pay-per-click program. Most Web sites and blogs, if they have reasonably good content and meet the search engine's terms of condition, are approved. As mentioned earlier in the chapter, there is a little work involved with setting up a pay-per-click program, but once things are setup, AdSense or any of the other programs do the rest. The most compelling aspect of pay-per-click programs is that they deliver contextually relevant ads. So if you start a blog about fitness, AdSense will place ads related to fitness on your blog. It's actually fun to watch because the ads will change based on the specific topic you're blogging about. If you write about running on one day, the ads will be for running related products, like treadmills, running shoes, and running apparel. If the topic is swimming two days later, the ads will change and focus on products like swimsuits, goggles, cruises, and sunscreen. AdSense does this by continually scanning blog entries and matching ads with keywords it finds.

Similar to affiliate programs, pay-per-click programs help people who put up special interest Web sites and blogs make money by selling access to the people they attract. Content-rich Web sites often place AdSense ads in multiple locations on their sites. For example, Tim Carter, a well-know columnist on home repair, has a Web site named Ask the Builder (www.askthebuilder.com). Information and instructions on all types of home building projects and repair are available on this Web site, as are links to areas that focus on specific topics, like air conditioning, cabinets, deck construction, lighting, and plumbing. Clicking any one of these areas brings up AdSense ads that deal with that specific area. All together, the site has hundreds of AdSense ads. Carter is able to do this and still attract large numbers of visitors because the information he provides is good and helpful. He might also believe that his ads, in a certain respect, add valuable content to the site. If someone is looking at the portion of his site that deals with how to construct a deck, he or she might actually appreciate seeing ads that point to Web sites where books and blueprints for building decks are available.

The one thing people should strictly avoid in participating in pay-per-click programs is trying to game the system by clicking ads on your own Web sites (to make yourself money) or asking your friends to click the ads. Google, Yahoo!, and the other providers of pay-per-click programs consider this to be "click-fraud" and have extremely sophisticated systems for detecting when this is happening. If you get caught doing this, you can be kicked out of a pay-per-click program, and once you get kicked out it is reportedly very difficult to be readmitted.

Direct Ads

The third way individuals and businesses make money online is through direct advertising programs. These ads tend to be banner ads, skyscraper ads (tall ads that run along the side of a Web page), or ads with pictures that are embedded in the content of a Web site or blog. If you run ads like these on your Web site or blog, you're paid a commission based on either the number of times an ad is clicked or the number of times it's seen (that is, the number of "impressions"). This type of advertising was more popular before affiliate programs and pay-per-click advertising caught on. Many Web site and blog owners shy away from banner ads in particular because they tend to be seen as more intrusive than text ads.

Similar to hooking up with an affiliate program, you can get involved with direct advertising in one of two ways. The first way is to contact an advertiser directly and negotiate the placement of ads. The advantage of doing this is that you eliminate the cut that AdSense or one of the facilitators of an affiliate program takes to deliver you ads. Many Web sites have links that say "Advertise Here" to encourage people to contact them directly. For example, on Ask the Builder's Web site, there is a link on the toolbar at the top of the site labeled "Advertise." This link provides detailed information about Ask the Builder's direct advertising program.

The second way to get involved in direct advertising is to work through a company that arranges direct advertising for online merchants. There are many companies that do this, including BurstMedia (www.burstmedia.com), DoubleClick (www.doubleclick.com), and Tribal Fusion (www.tribalfusion.com). An example of a Web site that is almost always displaying direct ads is Deal of the Day (www.dealoftheday.com).

The judgment call that Web site and blog owners have to make, as it pertains to affiliate programs, pay-per-click ads, and direct ads, is how much is enough. It's a delicate balancing act. As a Web site or blog owner, you want to maximize the earning potential of your site without driving away visitors. One of the nice things about the Internet is that the owner of a Web site or blog can track the traffic on the sites on a real-time basis. As a result, many people are constantly experimenting with the amount of advertising that's displayed on their sites and carefully monitoring how changes in the amount and types of advertising affect the number of visitors they attract.

Why "Free" Web Sites Are Popular

An understanding of how Internet advertising works answers a question that many people ask about the Internet. Why do so many Web sites provide the services they do for free? Blue Mountain (www.blue-mountain.com), for example, is a Web site that allows its users to send free e-Cards, create and print cards to be delivered in person, and do all kinds of other fun stuff for free. They don't even sell upgrades or premium products. There is no where on the Blue Mountain Web site where you can spend money.

So why does Blue Mountain do all of this for free? The reason is that free sites tend to attract users faster than sites that charge for their services, and the more visitors that Blue Mountain can get to its site, the more it can charge for advertising. Many of the Web's most popular companies, including MySpace and Facebook, are based largely on this model. By boosting its number of visitors, Blue Mountain can also attract higher-quality advertisers. The company currently displays ads for blue chip advertisers such as MetLife, Circuit City, PetSmart, and Disney.

E-Commerce

A fourth way that individuals and small businesses make money online is through e-commerce. E-commerce refers to the direct buying and selling of products and services online. Several of the Internet businesses we've highlighted in this book, including Wadee (children's toys and gift items) and Odd Ball Shoe Company (odd sized shoes), are e-commerce companies. They have Web sites that are online storefronts and utilize the Internet to sell their products.

There are various types of e-commerce companies. Some companies sell services. An example is onlc (www.onlc.com), a company that sells access to online training videos that help people learn computer software products like Microsoft Access and Excel. Other companies sell matchmaking services. TechStudents.com, for example, sells a service that matches people who need Web sites designed and similar services with technology-oriented college students who are looking for part-time work.

For e-commerce companies that sell products, there are two primary ways they go about it. Some companies, like Wadee, make their own products, warehouse them, and ship them to customers when they receive an order. Other companies utilize a process referred to as *drop-shipping*. Drop-shippers feature an online storefront but do not have any inventory. Instead, when they take an order, they pass it on to a wholesaler or manufacturer who fills the order and then ships it directly to the customer. The product is normally shipped in a box with the online retailer's name on it and the retailer's invoice inside, so it looks like it came directly from the online retailer. By utilizing this method, an online merchant earns a lower margin than it would if it controlled the entire process itself, but its costs are lower, too. It also doesn't get stuck with inventory that goes out of style or doesn't sell for some other reason. The system is not completely friction-free. The online retailer still has to offer customer support and deal with shipping complaints and returned items.

eBags (www.ebags.com), an e-commerce company that sells luggage, handbags, backpacks, and similar items, is an example of a drop-shipper. One of the most attractive aspects of eBag's online store is the sheer number of bags it has for sale—over 8,000. It's unlikely that eBags would carry so many bags if it had to maintain its own inventory and take the risk of getting caught with outdated products.

Most e-commerce companies do not participate in affiliate, pay-per-click programs, or direct advertising programs, opting instead to feature clean-looking Web sites that focus strictly on the products or services they have for sale. This isn't always the case, however. Buy.com, for example, is primarily an e-commerce Web site but almost always has other types of advertising prominently displayed on its site. The reverse also occurs. Some special interest Web sites and blogs that make most of their money on online advertising will have some e-commerce. Ask the Builder, for example, has an online store along with the content and advertising described earlier.

Subscription Services

A fifth way that individuals and businesses make money online is through subscription or monthly access services. These sites typically have specific services that they provide that have sufficient value that people in their niche markets are willing to pay for. Examples are companies that provide "members only" access to online games, music downloads, newsletters, and streaming video coverage of sporting events. For example, Rhapsody is an online music download site. For $14.99 per month, you can download an unlimited number of songs from Rhapsody's two million song library. The songs only remain available, however, while your subscription is current.

A common strategy among firms that charge subscription or access fees is to give away a basic version of whatever they offer for free, to attract visitors, and then sell access to upgraded versions of the service. An example is Box.net, a relatively new online company. Box.net provides online storage for documents, photos, video files, media clips, and any other type of digital file. There are three levels of participation in the company's business: Lite, Individual, and Business. The Lite service, which includes one gigabyte of storage, is free. The Individual service includes five gigabytes of storage for $7.95 per month. The Business service includes 15 gigabytes of storage for $19.85 per month.[5]

Interestingly, some of the subscription-based sites are very resilient in direct competition with sites that offer a similar service for free but include ads on their sites. An example is SmugMug (www.smugmug.com), an online photo sharing site. SmugMug charges $39.95 per year to store unlimited photos online. Other sites, like Shufferfly, Flickr, and WebShots, offer photo storage for free. Ostensibly, the reason SmugMug is able to charge a fee is that it offers higher levels of customer service and has a more user-friendly interface (in terms of how you view photos online) than its competitors. But the owners of SmugMug feel that its ability to charge goes beyond these obvious points. Some of the free sites have closed abruptly, and the users have lost photos. (Who wants to lose their photos?) SmugMug, because it charges, might be seen as more reliable and dependable for the long-term. In addition, the owners believe that when people pay for something, they innately assign a higher value to it. As a result, SmugMug users tend to treat the site with respect by posting attractive, high-quality photos that are in good taste. SmugMug's users appreciate this facet of the site, compared to the free sites, where unseemly photos often creep in.[6]

Quentin's Friends: Turning a Social Networking Site into a Money-Making Endeavor by Charging Users

During the late 1990s, Quentin English frequently fielded e-mail messages from friends who wanted help finding roommates and apartments in New York City. In early 2000, he decided to set up an online forum to more efficiently help his friends swap tips about apartments and living in the city.

The forum, called Quentin's Friends, started with about 25 people but quickly grew as Quentin's friends invited their friends to join the forum. By 2000, the number of members had swelled to about 5,000. For Quentin, this meant extra work, so he gradually started trying to make money on the site. He tried ads and several other ideas with only limited success. In 2004, he decided to start charging a subscription fee of $4.50 a month or $12.00 a year to participate in the site. Skeptics told him he'd be lucky to keep 5% of his participants, but about 25% agreed to pay. Today, the site is growing and is reportedly profitable. People exchange information about jobs, apartments, kitchen and computer equipment, reliable doctors, and other types of everyday interests and concerns. People can only join Quentin's Friends if they're invited by a current member, and they can get kicked out for inappropriate behavior or for giving out deceptive information.

Quentin acknowledges that his subscription approach was a gamble, given that people can get information about apartments, roommates, and similar things through free services like Craigslist.com. It's one more example of the multiple ways that people make money on the Internet when they provide a product or service for which someone is willing to pay.[7]

Other

There is a variety of other ways that individuals and businesses make money online. Redfin (www.redfin.com), for example, allows customers to buy and sell homes online and charges a commission on each real-estate transaction it brokers. Sermo (www.sermo.com), a social networking site for licensed physicians, makes money by monitoring discussions and determining how doctors feel about new drugs and then sells data reflecting aggregated trends. The names of the individual doctors, of course, are omitted, and the practice is fully disclosed to Sermo's members when they register.

Platforms That Help Freelancers Sell Their Products and Services Online

One exciting group of Internet businesses, which are increasing in prominence and use, are Web sites that serve as platforms to help freelancers sell their products or services online. There are many people who have full-time jobs and earn extra money on a "freelance" basis as a consultant, business plan writer, artist, photographer, or through some other means. Historically, a challenge these folks have had is getting the word out about their work. Many people are excellent photographers or Web site designers but have never made much extra money because they haven't found a practical way to connect with people who need what they do.

A growing number of Web sites are sprouting up to solve this exact problem. These sites not only help people earn extra income but in some cases have helped people start home businesses and transform a hobby or skill into a full-time job.

This section discusses two categories of Web sites that act as platforms to help freelancers and others sell their products and services.

General Web Sites That Help Freelancers Sell Their Work

There are a number of general or all-purpose Web sites that help freelancers find work. The largest and best-known sites in this category are Guru.com, Elance.com, and Sologig.com. The primary purpose of these sites is to match individuals or businesses that need work done with freelancers who specialize in a specific area. The breadth of specialties that these sites cover continues to grow. Guru.com, for example, claims that it has helped over 30,000 companies employ over 629,000 freelancers to do various jobs.[8] The jobs range from data entry to Web site design to installing kitchens.

Most of the sites are free to the employer and charge freelancers a monthly or yearly membership fee and a 6% to 10% commission on the money they earn. Some sites allow freelancers to bid on jobs, while others introduce companies to freelancers and allow the two parties to negotiate a price. Nearly all of the sites post ratings and reviews of freelancers provided by the companies they've worked for and vice versa, so there is a strong incentive on the part of everyone to perform. Although the sites do not indemnify the work of the freelancers, several of the sites will hold a company's money in escrow, and the freelancer is only paid when a job is completed satisfactorily. On some of the sites, YouTube videos of freelancers demonstrating their work are available. In most cases, you can also privately chat or instant message with freelancers without sharing personal contact information.

To get a good sense of what these sites are like, spend a few minutes browsing around Guru.com or Elance.com. Pay particular attention to the sheer number and variety of freelancers who are involved and the amount of money they've made. One of the biggest advantages of these sites, from a company's point of view, is that a freelancer can normally be "tried out" fairly inexpensively. So if you're an advertising or public relations firm, and you design logos for your clients, you can normally find someone on Guru.com or Elance.com to outsource this work for $200 or less. If you like the work the person does, you can use them for future jobs. If you don't like their work, the most you lose is $200 (or whatever the fee was). This logic makes it easy to understand why so many companies are opting to use freelancers to do work for them rather than taking a much larger risk by hiring additional employees.

The one thing that sites like Guru.com and Elance.com are not, and are not intended to be, are job sites like CareerBuilder.com. The matches they make are for project-based work, like copywriting an article or a book, designing a Web site, or photographing a wedding. In fact, the average contract handled by Guru.com is less than $700.[9] This aspect of Guru.com and similar sites is their biggest strength in the eyes of many freelancers. Freelancers are not typically looking for a full-time job, but are looking for ways to earn income by doing project-based work in their free time.

Specific Web Sites That Target Freelancers Who Work in Certain Areas

There are also Web sites that focus on specific types or categories of freelance work. A sample of these sites is shown in Table 8.2. Many of the sites have interfaces that resemble Guru.com and Elance.com. Their fee structures and setups vary. Freelance Switch (http://freelanceswitch.com) provides a directory of niche freelance sites like those shown in Table 8.1.

Table 8.2 A Sample of Web Sites That Target Freelancers Who Work in Certain Areas

Web Site	Area	Web Site Address
Altpick	Artists, illustrators, photographers	www.altpick.com
Design Crowd	Web site design	www.designcrowd.com
Proz	Translation services	www.proz.com
RentACoder	Software development	www.rentacoder.com
Writerlance	Freelance writing	www.writerlance.com

There is also a growing number of Web sites designed to help freelancers in another way. Instead of directly matching freelancers with companies, these sites provide a marketplace or storefront to help freelancers sell their products directly to the public. eBay is an obvious example. Another example is Etsy (www.etsy.com), mentioned earlier in the chapter, which is an online marketplace for the sales of handmade products. Etsy provides a platform for people who make crafts and similar products to display their work, and the Internet provides the leverage Etsy needs to reach a global audience. It also reconnects buyers with handmade items. Started in 2005, the company now has nearly 550,000 registered users, 60,000 of whom are individual artists selling more than 700,000 different handmade items.[10] There are 30 different categories of items listed on the Etsy Web site ranging from Accessories (aprons, belts, umbrellas) to Woodworking (carvings, clocks, home décor). Each Etsy freelancer is provided an Etsy store to sell his or her products. Kate Black and Karen Adelman are Etsy freelancers. Their Etsy stores can be seen at www.kateblack.etsy.com and www.kartdesign.etsy.com, respectively.

A similar example of a Web site that provides a platform for freelancers to make money is Zazzle.com. Zazzle is an online service that allows its customers to upload images that can be printed on T-shirts, stamps, posters, cards, coffee mugs, and a variety of other items. This approach allows freelancers to place digital images they've produced on products, like coffee mugs and posters, and resell them at craft shows and through other outlets. In addition, Zazzle maintains an inventory of digital images that are posted on its Web site, many of which are provided to the company by freelance photographers. If an image provided by a freelancer is used to create a T-shirt, poster, coffee mug, or other item by a third party, the creator of the image is paid up to a 17% royalty.

Summary

It's important to know the most common ways that businesses and individuals make money online. Almost all businesses now have Internet strategies, so the extent to which the various ways of making money online are appropriate for a business is an essential issue to discern. It will also become increasingly important to know how to utilize the Internet to make various forms of a business more effective. For example, a growing number of businesses are utilizing the services of Web sites like Guru.com and Elance.com to find good people to complete project-based work.

The final chapter of the book focuses on the myth that it's easy to start a business, but it's difficult and stressful to grow one. This myth is a tough one to grapple with because it sometimes is true. As indicated in the chapter, growing a business can be a joy or a nightmare—it all depends on how the process is managed. In the chapter, we tackle the most important issues pertaining to firm growth and lay out a roadmap for how to approach this important topic.

Endnotes

[1] Internet World Stats home page, http://www.internetworldstats.com (accessed October 21, 2001).

[2] "U.S. Retail E-Commerce: Entering the Multi-Channel Era," eMarketer, http://www.emarketer.com (accessed October 21, 2007).

[3] Rachael King, "Make Some Noise," *BusinessWeek SmallBiz*, August/September 2007, 71.

[4] eBay home page, http://www.ebay.com (accessed October 21, 2007).

[5] Box.net home page, http://www.box.net (accessed October 21, 2007).

[6] nPost home page, Don MacAskill, CEO of SmugMug, http://www.npost.com (accessed October 21, 2007).

[7] David Enrich, "Turning an Online Community into a Business," *The Wall Street Journal*, February 27, 2007, B8.

[8] Guru.com home page, http://www.guru.com (accessed October 25. 2007).

[9] James M. Connolly, "Putting Individual Contractors to Work," Microsoft home page, http://www.microsoft.com (accessed October 25, 2007).

[10] Etsy home page, http://www.etsy.com (accessed October 25, 2007).

Myth No. 9:
It's Easy to Start a Business, But It's Difficult and Stressful to Grow One

Truth No. 9:
Businesses Can Be Grown Profitably and Enjoyably

Introduction

A fear that many prospective business owners have is that once they get their businesses started, they won't be able to grow them successfully. It's easy to understand where this fear comes from. There is a prevailing notion that successful businesses are growth businesses, which has been bolstered by common phrases such as, "If you're not moving forward, you're moving backwards," and "Businesses either grow, or they die." There are also signals that remind us of just how difficult growing a business can be. Think about the number of times that we've all heard about businesses that have downsized or laid off employees. While there may be many reasons for those events, it's easy to infer that these businesses weren't able to sustain their growth. There are also sobering statistics that pertain to business growth. For example, Chris Zook, an expert on firm growth, has found that over a 10-year period only 1 in 10 businesses achieve more than a modest level of sustained and profitable growth (defined as 5.5% or more per year).[1] Reading that statistic would cause any prospective business owner to pause and think, "Wow, if only 1 out of 10 *existing* businesses grows by more than 5.5% per year, what chance does a *new* firm have?"

The reality is that if that you have a business that meets a defined need, and are a capable owner, in most instances you can grow your business profitably and enjoyably. It doesn't happen by happenstance, however. Growing a business successfully takes preparation, good management, and an awareness of the key issues involved. It also takes a business owner with a high degree of self-awareness and a strong, consistent sense of the type of business that he or she wants to have. Growing a business can be a joy or a nightmare. There are many businesses that have started, grown prudently, and are thriving, returning to their owners just the sort of lives they had hoped for. Sadly, there are also many businesses that have done just the opposite—they've started, grown either too slowly or too quickly, and have failed, leaving their owners financially and emotionally damaged. In most cases, these businesses had no plan for growth, and their owners didn't try to build their companies in a focused and purposeful manner.

The key to keeping the myth described in this chapter from coming true is to take determined steps to prevent it from happening. All businesses would rather grow profitably and enjoyably rather than in a difficult and stressful manner.

Improper growth can also ruin a business. For example, some businesses start slow and then get a string of large orders. If they're not careful, they can over commit and find themselves struggling to fill the orders and manage their cash flows in ways that allow them to regularly pay their employees. Similarly, early success can cause a business to become overconfident and hire too many people or lease too much manufacturing or office space, resulting in financial hardship. It's easy to err in either direction, which makes it doubly important to remain vigilant and follow a growth plan.

To discuss these important topics and further dispel the myth that it's easy to start a business but difficult and stressful to grow one, this chapter is divided into three parts. The first part focuses on preparing for growth. The second part focuses on managing growth. The third part describes the most common strategies businesses use to grow their firms.

Preparing for Growth

While there is some trial-and-error involved in starting and growing any business, the degree to which a firm prepares for its future growth has a direct bearing on its level of success. Many of the early decisions that a business makes, such as whether it will focus on a single product or become a multi-product firm, have an influence on the nature of its growth. This section focuses on three issues that are important as a business starts and prepares itself for growth. These issues are:

- Appreciating the nature of business growth
- Determining a business's core strengths and capabilities
- Planning for growth

Appreciating the Nature of Business Growth

The first issue that helps business owners prepare for growth is to gain an appreciation of the nature of business growth. Not knowing much about business growth, including the full range of outcomes that can occur, might cause a well-intended business owner to make decisions that cripple or ruin his or her business. The best way for a business owner to learn about growth is to access resources described throughout the book, such as talking to a SCORE advisor, attending a class on business growth hosted by a Small Business Development Center, or finding a mentor. Many businesses also form a Board of Advisors, which is a panel of experts who are asked by a business's owner to provide counsel and advice on an ongoing basis.

The first thing for a business owner to appreciate about growth is that not all businesses have the potential to be aggressive growth companies. The businesses that have the potential to grow the fastest over a sustained period of time are ones that solve a significant problem or have a major impact on their customers' productivity or lives. This is why the lists of fast-growing firms are often dominated by healthcare and technology companies. These companies have the potential to make the biggest impact on their customers' businesses or lives. This point is affirmed by contrasting the sporting goods industry with the biotechnology industry. From 2004 to 2006, the average sporting goods store in the United States grew by 3.3%, while the average biotechnology company grew by 13.1%.[2] While there is nothing wrong with starting and owning a sporting goods store, it's important to have a realistic outlook of how fast the business will likely grow. Even though an individual sporting goods store might get off to a fast start, as it gets larger, its annual growth will normally start to reflect its industry's norms.

The second thing that is important for a business owner to appreciate about growth is that businesses can grow too fast. Many businesses start fast and never let up, which is stressful for everyone involved. Other businesses start, grow at a measured pace, and then experience a sudden upswing in orders and have difficultly keeping up. This scenario can transform a business with satisfied customers and employees into a chaotic workplace with people scrambling to push the business's product out the door as quickly as possible. The way to prevent this from happening is to recognize when to put the brakes on and have the courage to do it. This set of circumstances played out early in the life of The Pampered Chef, the company that sells kitchen utensils through home parties. Just about the time the company was gaining serious momentum, it realized that it didn't have enough inventory to serve what it expected to be a busy Christmas season. This reality posed a serious dilemma. It couldn't instantly increase its inventory (its vendors were all low), yet it didn't want to discourage its home consultants from making sales or signing up new consultants. One option was to institute a recruiting freeze (on new home consultants), which would slow the rate of sales. Doris Christopher, the company's founder, remembers asking others for advice. Most advised against instituting a recruiting freeze, arguing that the lifeblood of any direct sales organization is to sign up new recruits. In the end, the company decided to institute the freeze and slowed its sales enough to fill all orders on time during the holiday season. The freeze was lifted the following January, and the number of Pampered Chef recruits soared. Reflecting on the decision, Doris Christopher later wrote:

> *"Looking back, the recruiting freeze augmented our reputation with our sales force, customers, and vendors. People saw us as an honest company that was trying to do the right thing and not overestimating our capabilities."*[3]

Other businesses have faced similar dilemmas and have sometimes made the right call and sometimes haven't. The overarching point is that growth must be handled with kid gloves. A business can only grow as fast as its infrastructure allows (a subject we talk more about later). A list of indicators that a business is growing too fast in provided in the following bulleted list.

- Borrowing money to pay for routine operating expenses.
- Extremely tight profit margins.
- Over-stretched staff.
- Quality is slipping.
- Customer complaints are up.
- Employees dread coming to work.
- Productivity is falling.
- The business's accountants are starting to worry.

The third thing it's important for a business owner to appreciate about growth is that business success doesn't always scale. What this means is that the very thing that makes a business successful might suffer as the result of growth. For example, Wadee, a company talked about throughout this book, sells hand-made gifts and toys for children. It would be hard for Wadee to grow quickly and still produce hand-made products. There might also be an upward limit on the number of people who are willing to pay extra for hand-made goods. To accelerate its growth, Wadee could start selling machine-made children's gifts and toys along with its hand-made products. But it would then lose its distinctiveness and cease being what it once was.

Similarly, businesses that are based on providing high levels of customer service often don't scale or grow well. An investment brokerage service, for example, that initially provided high levels of customer service can quickly evolve into providing standard or even substandard service as it adds customers, opens new offices, adds new product lines, and starts automating key functions. Its initial customers might find that it's harder to get individualized service than it once was and start viewing the company as just another ho-hum business.

There is also a category of businesses that sell high-end or specialty products that earn high margins. These businesses typically sell their products through venues where customers prioritize quality over price. These businesses can grow but only at a measured pace. If they grow too quickly, they can lose the "exclusivity" they are trying to project or can damage their special appeal.

The Case Against Quick Growth: Timbuk2's Short-Lived Partnership with CompUSA

In early 2003, Mark Dwight, the CEO of Timbuk2, the San Francisco-based manufacturer of urban shoulder bags, was on the top of the world. The company had just inked a deal with CompUSA to carry its bags, and it looked as if it had caught a big break. Impressive company growth was nearly assured for some time to come.

Yet just three months later, Dwight had second thoughts. It wasn't the sales. Sales were booming. But financially, Timbuk2 was being squeezed by the relationship. CompUSA's slim margins and high-volume demand were difficult for Timbuk2 to cope with. In addition, Dwight became increasingly worried that selling through a mainstream retailer would change how consumers viewed his company. He wanted to see his company increase sales, but he didn't want it to lose its quirkiness and unique appeal either.

So Dwight cancelled the CompUSA deal and refocused Timbuk2. In refocusing the company, he compared it to Coach, a company that sells primarily through specialty stores. Specialty stores, like the Sharper Image and the Apple Computer Store, appeal to consumers who prioritize quality and brand image over price. This attribute of specialty stores allows vendors like Timbuk2 to earn higher margins (than they would earn at a big-box retailer like CompUSA), which compensates for lower-volume sales.

The results of Dwight's decision have been impressive. Although Timbuk2 missed its chance for fast growth, sales are up, and the company has an increasingly attractive product line featuring items that are sold online and through specialty stores throughout the United States.

Determining a Business's Core Strengths and Capabilities

The second issue that helps business owners prepare for growth is to clearly identify their core strengths and capabilities. While this recommendation may seem self-evident, it continues to surprise us how many businesses aren't sure of what their most important strengths and capabilities are. The reason this topic is so important is that a business achieves healthy growth when it matches its strengths with opportunities. If a business doesn't know what its strengths are, it can easily stray into areas where it finds itself at a competitive disadvantage. This happened to Amazon.com early in its life as a company. Just months after it announced that it intended to become "a place where you can buy anything for anyone," Amazon laid off 15% of its workforce and started eliminating product lines under the slogan "Get the Crap Out." The company quickly realized that it was competing in areas that were not well-matched with its strengths, and its competitors had a decided advantage.[4]

The way successful businesses typically evolve is to start by selling a product or service that is consistent with their core strengths and capabilities and increase sales by incrementally moving into areas that are different from, but are related to, their core strengths and capabilities. Apple is a good example. It utilized its core strengths and capabilities in the areas of technology and design to create the Macintosh and its iMac line of computers and is now using those same strengths and capabilities to produce MP3 players (the iPod) and digital phones (the iPhone). In fact, Steve Jobs, Apple's co-founder and CEO, has been quoted as saying Apple is as proud of the things it doesn't make as the things it does. All of the company's products have fit within the scope of its unique strengths and capabilities.

LA Gear: How Straying from Its Core Strengths Nearly Cost a Firm Everything

For LA Gear, the late 1980s were golden. The company developed a core strength in designing and selling shoes with a distinctive "hip" Los Angeles style, and the shoes were a hit. It produced a line of "Valley Girls" sneakers for teen girls and young women. The shoes were made of denim and patent leather and were adorned with feminine fringes. Then, in the mid-1980s, the company created children's shoes with small lights in the heels that blinked when the walker's soles hit the ground. The shoes, dubbed L.A. Lights, flew off the shelves. The company's sales increased from $11 million in 1985 to $820 million in 1990. The company became a Wall Street darling, and its share price increased from $3 per share in 1987 to $50 per share two years later. But just as quickly as LA Gear heated up, it turned cold. The company filed for Chapter 11 bankruptcy protection in January 1998. What went wrong? Three things—all related to growth.

First, instead of focusing its efforts on making its core products better, rapid growth was LA Gear's first priority. When its leaders found an opportunity to expand, they pursued the opportunity, regardless of the relationship of the opportunity to the company's core strengths and capabilities. Second, in its thirst for growth, LA Gear quickly moved beyond producing shoes for teen girls and young women and rolled out a full line of sneakers to appeal to a broad spectrum of customers. Without changing its brand, which most people still associated with girls, the company was now trying to be all things to all people. Quality and timeliness of delivery started to suffer. Finally, LA Gear found that a company that lives by the notion of "cool" can also die by the notion of "cool." By failing to change its image and develop additional core strengths before it branched out, the company produced products that just didn't sell. Most people still saw LA Gear as a company that was good at making feminine-looking shoes for young girls regardless of how many markets it entered. As a result, by 1991, LA Gear had 12 million shoes in its warehouses that nobody wanted. The company still exists today but has never fully recovered from these missteps.[5]

Planning For Growth

The third thing that a business owner can do to prepare for growth is to establish growth-related plans. This task involves a firm thinking ahead and anticipating the type and amount of growth it wants to achieve.

The process of writing a general business plan greatly assists in developing growth-related plans. A business plan normally includes a detailed forecast of a firm's first three to five years of sales along with an operations plan that describes the resources the business will need to meet its projections. Even though the business will invariably change during its first three to five years, it's still good to have a plan. Many businesses periodically revise their business plans and allow them to help guide their growth-related decisions.

It's also important for a business to determine, as early as possible, the strategies for growth that it will try to employ. For example, Proactiv, the acne medicine company discussed in several chapters of this book, is a single-product company and has grown by steadily increasing its domestic sales, introducing its product into foreign markets, and by encouraging nontraditional users of acne medicine, like adult males, to use the product. Proactiv's decision to stick with one product and to avoid growing through initiatives like acquisitions and licensing has allowed the company to focus on marketing and building its brand. Similarly, Cranium, the board game company discussed in Chapter 7, has grown rapidly but made the decision early on to avoid the temptation to simply take its flagship Cranium game and develop "age appropriate" versions of it. Instead, each of the 14 games the company has developed has been built from the ground up and has been extensively tested within their age groups. For example, Cadoo is a board game for kids seven years old and older. The game fits in a backpack and is designed for two players (instead of four, like the original Cranium) given that kids normally have only one friend over at a time.[6]

On a more personal level, a business owner should step back and measure the company's growth plans against his or her personal goals and aspirations. The old adage, "Be careful what you wish for," is as true in business as it is in other areas of life. For example, if a business has the potential to grow rapidly, the owner should know what to expect if the fast-growth route is chosen. Fast-growth normally implies a quick pace of activity, a rapidly rising overhead, and a total commitment in terms of time and attention on the part of the business owners. The upside is that if the business is successful, the owner will normally do very well financially. The tradeoffs implied by this scenario are acceptable to some business owners and aren't to others. If a person is starting a business to improve his or her quality of life, running a fast-growth firm might not be worth the sacrifices involved. A person in this situation might deliberately throttle back a business's growth potential in exchange for more leisure time and a less stressful life.

Managing Growth

Many business owners are caught off guard by the challenges involved with growing their companies. One would think that if a business got off to a good start, steadily increased its sales, and started making money, things would get progressively easier for the business owner. In many instances, just the opposite occurs. As a business increases its sales, its pace of activity quickens, its resource needs increase, and the owner usually finds himself or herself busier than ever. Major challenges can also occur. For example, a business might project its next year's sales and realize it will need more people and additional equipment to handle the increased workload. The new equipment might need to be purchased and the new people hired and trained before the increased business generates additional income. It's easy to imagine a business owner tossing and turning in bed at night trying to figure out how that will all work out.

The reality is that a company must actively and carefully manage its growth for it to expand in a healthy and enjoyable manner. As a business grows and becomes better known, there are normally more opportunities that present themselves, but there are more things that can go wrong too. Many potential problems and heartaches can be avoided by prudently managing the growth process. This section focuses on two topics regarding how to manage growth: knowing and managing the stages and challenges of growth.

Knowing and Managing the Stages of Growth

The majority of businesses go through a discernable set of stages referred to as the *organizational life cycle*. The stages, pictured in Figure 9.1, include introduction, early growth, continuous growth, maturity, and decline. Each stage must be managed differently. It's important for business owners to be familiar with these stages, along with the unique opportunities and challenges that each stage entails. The introduction, early growth, and continuous growth stages are discussed in the following sections.[7]

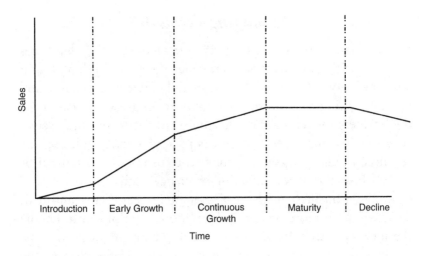

Figure 9.1 *Stages of growth*

Introduction

This is the start-up phase where a business determines what its core strengths and capabilities are and starts selling its initial products or services. It's a very "hands-on" phase for the owner who is normally involved in every aspect of the day-to-day life of the business. The business is typically very nonbureaucratic with no (or few) written rules and procedures. The main goal of the business is to get off to a good start and to try to gain momentum in the marketplace.

The main challenges for a business in the introduction stage are to make sure the initial product or service is right and to start laying the groundwork for building a larger organization. It's important not to rush things. This sentiment is affirmed by April Singer, the founder of Rufus Shirts, a company that makes high-end shirts for men. Before growing her business beyond the introduction stage, Singer made sure that her unique approach for making men's shirts worked and that it resonated in the marketplace:

> *"Before growing too much too fast, I wanted to spend two seasons making sure that the concept worked, that I shipped well, and that consumers liked the product. They did."*[8]

This affirmation gave Singer the confidence to expand her business and move into a more aggressive growth mode. In regard to laying the groundwork to build a larger organization, many businesses use the introduction stage to try different concepts to see what works and what doesn't, recognizing that trial-and-error gets harder as a business grows. It's important to document what works and start thinking about how the company's success can be replicated when the owner isn't present or when the business expands beyond its original location. Betsy Ludlow, the founder of Slim and Tone, a fitness center for women, documented nearly every move she made during the early days of her business. This practice paid off when Slim and Tone moved into its early growth phase and became a franchise organization. Reflecting on her experience, Ludlow recalls:

> "I documented everything. When I bought something, I kept receipts. I made notes of every step I went through to open my first club. By the third club, I realized, hmmm...I have material to start putting together the training curriculum and operating manuals so that someone could do exactly what I just did. That's how I turned it into a franchise concept." [9]

Early Growth

A business's early growth stage is normally characterized by increasing sales and heightened complexity. The business is normally still focused on its initial product or service but is trying to increase its market share and might have related products in the works. The initial formation of policies and procedures take place, and the process of running the business will start to consume more of the owner's time and attention.

For a business to be successful in this stage, two important things must take place. First, the owner of the business must start transitioning from his or her role as the hands-on supervisor of every aspect of the business to a more managerial role. As articulated by Michael E. Gerber in his excellent book *The E-Myth Revisited*, the owner must start working "on the business" rather than "in the business." [10] The basic idea is that early in the life of a business, the owner is typically directly involved in building the product or delivering the service that the business provides. As the business moves into the early growth stage, the owner must let go of that role and spend more time learning how to manage and build the business. If the owner isn't willing to make this transition or doesn't know that it needs to be made, the business will never grow beyond the owner's ability to directly supervise everything that takes place, and the business's growth will eventually stall. After all, even the most energetic people have limits on how much they can do.

The second thing that must take place for a business to be successful in the early growth stage is that increased formalization must take place. The business has to start developing policies and procedures that tell employees how to run it when the owner or other top managers aren't present. This is how a McDonald's restaurant runs so well when it's staffed by what appears to be a group of teenagers. The employees are simply following the policies and procedures that were originally written down by Ray Kroc, McDonald's founder, and have been added to and improved upon over the years. An early growth stage business will not develop policies and procedures as elaborate as McDonald's, but it must start formalizing how it achieves its success. This task was clearly on the mind of Emily Levy, the founder of EBL Coaching, a tutoring service for children who are struggling in school or trying to overcome disabilities, when she was asked by Ladies Who Launch early in the life of her business her growth plans:

> "My future goals include continuing to spread EBL Coaching's programs nationally, using our proprietary materials and self-contained multi-sensory methods. I have already developed a series of workbooks, called 'Strategies for Success,' addressing specific study skills strategies, that are being used in a number of schools across the country. The real challenge will be figuring out how to replicate our programs while maintaining our high quality of teaching and personalized approach." [11]

Levy was clearly trying to envision how her business would replicate its initial success in other locations. This is a task that all business owners need to do during the early stages of growth.

Continuous Growth Stage

As a business moves beyond its early growth stage and its pace of growth accelerates, the need for structure and formalization increases. The resource requirements of the business are usually a major concern, along with the ability of the owner and manager to take the firm to the next level. Often, the business will start developing new products and services and will expand to new markets. Smaller firms may be acquired, and the business might start partnering with other firms. When handled correctly, the business's expansion will be in areas that are related to its core strengths and capabilities, or it will develop new strengths and capabilities to complement its activities.

The toughest decisions are typically made in the continuous growth stage. One tough decision is whether the owner of the business and the current management team have the experience and ability to take the firm any further. This scenario played out for Rachael Ashwell, the founder of Shabby Chic, a home furnishing business. Ashwell expanded her company to five separate locations, inked a licensing deal with Target, wrote five how-to books related to her business, and hosted her own television show on the Style Network before she concluded that her business had stalled. Her choice was to continue running the business or find more experienced management to grow it further.

She opted for the latter, and Shabby Chic is growing again.[12] Another decision that often is made is whether to continue to grow a business or sell it to a larger company. This is often a very personal and difficult decision for a business owner.

The importance of developing policies and procedures increases during the continuous growth stage. It's also important for a business to develop a formal organizational structure and determine clear lines of delegation throughout the business. Although "formalization" is a term that is often frowned upon by business owners who want to free themselves from the trappings of Corporate America, well-developed policies and procedures lead to order, which typically makes the process of growing a business more organized, enjoyable, and successful.

Challenges of Growth

There is a consistent set of challenges that affects all stages of a firm's growth. The challenges typically become more acute as a business grows, but a business's owner and managers also become more savvy and experienced with the passage of time. The challenges illustrate that no firm grows in a competitive vacuum. As a business grows and takes market share away from rival firms, there will be a certain amount of retaliation that takes place. This is an aspect of competition that a business owner needs to be aware of and plan for. Competitive retaliation normally increases as a business grows and becomes a bigger threat to its rivals.

The following is a discussion of the four most common challenges of firm growth.

Cash Flow Management

As a firm grows, it normally requires an increasing amount of cash to service its customers. In addition, it must carefully manage its cash reserves to make sure it has enough money in the bank to meet its payroll and cover its short-term obligations. There are many colorful anecdotes about business owners who have had to rush to a bank and get a second mortgage on their houses to cover their business's payroll. This set of events usually occurs when a business takes on too much work, and its customers are slow to pay. A business can literally have a million dollars in accounts receivable but not be able to meet a $25,000 payroll. This is why almost any book you pick up about growing a business stresses the importance of properly managing your cash flow.

Growth usually increases rather than decreases the challenges involved with cash flow management because an increase in sales means more money is flowing into and out of the business. Some businesses deal with potential cash flow shortfalls by establishing a line of credit at a bank or by raising investment capital. Other businesses deliberately restrict the pace of their growth to avoid cash flow challenges. The latter option is preferred by Dave

Schwartz, the founder of Rent-A-Wreck, a discount car rental company, who grew his firm through earnings rather than debt or investment capital. Commenting on this issue, Schwartz said:

> *"One of the main things I tell people starting out is not to grow too quickly. Often it's better to grow slowly, and when you do expand, try to grow with cash flows [meaning grow with your own money]."*[13]

Price Stability

If a new business grows at the expense of a competitor's market share, price competition can set in. For example, if a new video store opens near a Blockbuster store, and the new store starts to erode Blockbuster's market share, Blockbuster will probably fight back by running promotions or lowering its price. This type of scenario places a new firm in a difficult predicament and illustrates why it's so important to start a business by selling a differentiated product in a niche market. There is no good way for a small firm to compete toe-to-toe against a much larger rival on price. The best thing for the small firm to do is avoid price competition by serving a different market and by serving that different market very well.

Quality Control

One of the most difficult challenges that businesses encounter as they grow is maintaining high levels of quality and customer service. As a firm grows, it handles more service requests and paperwork and contends with an increasing number of prospects, customers, vendors, and other stakeholders. If a business can't build its infrastructure fast enough to handle the increased activity, quality and customer service will usually suffer. What happens to many businesses is that they run into the classic chicken-and-egg quandary. It's hard to justify hiring additional employees or leasing more office space until the need is present, but if the business waits until the need is present, it usually won't have enough employees or office space to properly service new customers.

There is no easy way to resolve this type of quandary other than to recognize that it may take place and to plan for it the best you can. Many businesses find innovative and inexpensive ways to expand their capacity to try to avoid shortfalls in quality control or customer service. An example is an online merchant that utilizes drop-shipping rather than maintaining its own inventory as discussed in Chapter 8. Another example is a firm that utilizes temporary workers to plug resource gaps created by faster than expected growth.

Capital Constraints

Although many businesses are started fairly inexpensively, the need for capital is typically the most prevalent in the early growth and continuous growth stages of the organizational life cycle. The amount of capital required varies widely among businesses. Some businesses, like restaurant chains, might need considerable capital to hire employees, construct buildings, and purchase equipment. If they can't raise the capital they need, their growth will be stymied.

Most businesses, regardless of their industry, need capital from time to time to invest in growth-enabling projects. Their ability to raise capital, whether it's through internally generated funds, through a bank, or from investors, will determine in part whether their growth plans proceed.

Want to Minimize the Amount of Capital Needed to Grow? Follow the Lead of CD Baby and Act Like a Hedgehog

CD Baby, an online music store, has the largest catalog of music in the world, even though you've probably never heard of the majority of its musicians. Since its founding in 1997, CD Baby has maintained a laser-like focus on its primary mission—to provide a way for independent musicians to sell their music at a profit. The results have been impressive. Over 100,000 independent musicians now sell their music through the CD Baby Web site.

One thing that is extraordinary about CD Baby is that with the exception of partnering with Apple's iTunes and the other online music services, CD Baby has built its business without expanding beyond its core service. Although the company gets inquiries nearly every week about potential business opportunities, it has never bit on any of the offers. Derek Sivers, the company's founder and CEO, likes to use the fable of the Hedgehog and the Fox to explain why.

The tale of the "Hedgehog and the Fox" was written by Isaiah Berlin. Because he is sly, cunning, and strong, everyone thinks that the fox is better than the hedgehog. All the lowly hedgehog knows how to do is one thing—curl up in a ball, with its spikes out, to deter intruders. The ironic thing is that no matter what the fox does, and no matter how many of its 100 tricks it tries to use, the hedgehog always wins, because it knows how to do one thing particularly well—roll up in a ball and stick its spikes out. Sivers was reminded of this story while reading Jim Collin's book *Good to Great*. In *Good to Great*, Collins says businesses that are successful over the long-haul are like hedgehogs—they find their niche or market space and learn how to do one thing exceptionally well.

Sivers has taken Collin's advice to heart and has centered CD Baby's growth philosophy on one thing—being an online music store. The company is successful and continues to grow. An added benefit is that by focusing on one thing and executing it particularly well, Sivers has built his company less expensively than similarly sized companies that have more multifaceted product lines.[14]

Growth Strategies

The practical side of growth is the actual strategies that businesses employ to grow their companies. It's helpful for business owners to be acquainted with the breadth of growth-related strategies that are available, so they can select the strategy or strategies that make the most sense at a certain point in time in light of their individual situations.

This section discusses the most common strategies for growth utilized by expanding businesses. The strategies are divided into internal growth strategies and external growth strategies, as shown in Figure 9.2 and discussed here.

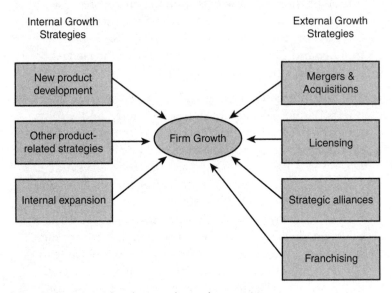

Figure 9.2 *Internal and external growth strategies*

Internal Growth Strategies

Internal growth strategies involve efforts taken within the firm itself, such as new product development, other product-related strategies, and international expansion. Almost all firms start by featuring internal growth, and many firms, such as Flavorx, Proactiv, and Daisy Rock Guitar, stick with this strategy as they grow. A firm that features internal growth relies on its own strengths and capabilities to spur its growth, rather than going into the marketplace and creating growth through an acquisition or a strategic alliance. The full range of internal growth strategies available to businesses is shown in Table 9.1.

Table 9.1 Internal Growth Strategies

Growth Strategy	Description
New product development	Involves designing, producing, and selling new products or services as a means of increasing firm revenues and profitability.
Improving an existing product or service	Often, a business can increase its revenue by improving an existing product or service—enhancing quality, making it larger or smaller, making it more convenient to use, improving its durability, or making it more up-to-date.
Increasing the market penetration of an existing product or service	A market penetration strategy involves actions taken to increase the sales of a product or service through greater marketing efforts or through increased production capacity and efficiency.
Extending product lines	A product line extension strategy involves making additional versions of a product so that it will appeal to different clientele or making related products to sell to the same clientele.
Geographic expansion	Many businesses grow by simply expanding from their original location to additional geographic sites.
International expansion	Growing a business by expanding its sales to international markets.

Many businesses prefer internal growth because it typically leads to an incremental, even-paced approach to growth. For example, a company like Shabby Chic, the home furnishing business introduced earlier, is growing by opening stores and selling its products through distributors. By growing in this manner, the company can control its pace of growth and time its store openings and new distribution agreements to coincide with the resources it has available. It's also easier for a business to control its culture by growing through internal means. If a company grows by adding employees as new products come online, it can socialize the employees into its culture. In contrast, if a firm grows via an external strategy, such as an acquisition, it will have employees who have been raised in different corporate cultures and will normally have a more difficult task creating cohesion among its employees.

The primary downside of internal growth is that it tends to be a slow form of business growth. While a slow, deliberate approach to growth has many advantages, in some industries, relying strictly on internal growth does not permit a firm to develop sufficient economies of scale or broaden its product offerings fast enough to remain competitive. An example is Google. Google has completed a number of acquisitions, like its recent acquisition of YouTube, to stay ahead of Yahoo! and Microsoft in online search, pay-per-click advertising, and related activities. Google's industry is moving too fast for it to develop all of its new products and services internally.

External Growth Strategies

External growth strategies rely on establishing relationships with other firms, such as mergers, acquisitions, strategic alliances, licensing agreements, and franchising. It is increasingly common for businesses to utilize one or more external growth strategies as early as the early growth stage of its organizational life cycle. The full range of external growth strategies available to businesses is shown in Table 9.2.

Table 9.2   External Growth Strategies

Growth Strategy	Description
Merger	A merger is the pooling of interests to combine two or more firms into one.
Acquisition	An acquisition is the outright purchase of one firm by another.
Licensing	Licensing is the granting of permission by one company to another company to use a specific form of its intellectual property in exchange for a flat fee or royalty payments.
Strategic alliance	A strategic alliance is a partnership between two or more firms that is developed to achieve a specific goal.
Franchising	Franchising is a form of business organization in which a firm that already has a successful product or service (franchisor) licenses its trademark and method of doing business to other businesses (franchisees) in exchange for an initial franchise fee and an ongoing royalty.

A business can normally grow faster through external growth than internal growth because it immediately adds a product or capability that might have taken months or years to develop internally. For example, when eBay acquired PayPal, it acquired PayPal's proprietary electronic payments system, something PayPal worked diligently to perfect over a period of several years. Similarly, by forming a strategic alliance, a firm can tap into the resources of its alliance partner and reach new markets without having to build out its own infrastructure. For example, many American food companies have strategic alliances with large European food companies, like Nestlé, to gain access to their European distribution networks.

The primary downside of external growth is that by relying on other firms to help develop its growth, a business losses some of its flexibility and decision autonomy. It also complicates its business and runs the risk of joining forces with an unreliable partner. The net result of engaging in external growth is usually to speed up a business's pace of growth. As a business's pace of growth increases, the challenges of growth, such as cash flow management, quality control, and capital constraints, are usually exacerbated.

Many businesses blend internal and external strategies for growth as they pass through the stages of growth and expand their businesses. The important thing to remember as a business owner is that you should select the means of growth that is best for you and your company, given the conditions you face.

Summary

There is no topic more deserving of study on the part of a business owner than how to successfully grow a firm. It is not uncommon for a business to start successfully, provide an initial period of satisfaction and joy for its owners, and then turn sour as the owner struggles with the pressures and challenges imposed by growth. The good news is that it doesn't have to turn out that way for you. If you start a business and decide to grow it beyond the scope of a small firm, reread this chapter periodically and seek out mentors and other forms of assistance and advice. Businesses can be grown successfully, but it does take perseverance, hard work, and a willingness to make tough choices.

As you glance down and realize that this is the final paragraph of this book, we'd like to leave you with one final piece of advice. There are some books that will tell you that starting a business is the smartest thing you can do—regardless of your alternatives. We hope we haven't conveyed that message. Starting a business is the right thing for some people, and it's the wrong thing for others. What we do believe, however, is that you shouldn't let the myths discussed in this book make your mind up for you. Our guess is that if you picked up this book and spent the time to read it, you're a capable, passionate, and responsible person. If starting a business is the right decision for you, you can do it!

Endnotes

1 Chris Zook, "Find Your Next Core Business," TheStreet.com, http://www.thestreet.com (accessed November 2, 2007).

2 IBIS World, http://www.ibisworld.com (accessed on November 4, 2007).

3 Christopher, *The Pampered Chef*, 166 (see chap. 4, n. 6).

4 Bruce R. Barringer and R. Duane Ireland, *Entrepreneurship: Successfully Launching New Ventures* (Upper Saddle River, NJ: Prentice-Hall, 2006).

5 W. Joyce, N. Nohria, and B. Robinson, *What Really Works* (New York: HarperBusiness, 2003); D. Darlin, "Getting Beyond a Market Niche," *Forbes*, November 22, 1993, 106.

6 "Cranium Builds on Success to Enter Toy Category," Cranium Press Release (May 2006); J. Bick, "Inside the Smartest Little Company in America," *Inc.*, January 2002.

7 Ladies Who Launch, accessed November 5, 2007 (see chap. 1, n. 4).

8 Ladies Who Launch, accessed November 5, 2007 (see chap. 1, n. 4).

9 Ladies Who Launch, accessed November 5, 2007 (see chap. 1, n. 4).

10 Michael E. Gerber, *The E-Myth Revisited* (New York: HarperCollins, 2004).

11 Ladies Who Launch, accessed November 5, 2007 (see chap. 1, n. 4).

12 Chris Penttila, "When Success Isn't Enough," Entrepreneur.com, http://www.entrepreneur.com (accessed November 4, 2007).

13 D. Bartholomew, "The Perfect Pitch," *Priority*, December/January, 2004.

14 Greg Galant and Derek Sivers, "VV Show #19—Derek Sivers of CD Baby," Venture Voice: Entertaining Entrepreneurship, http://www.venturevoice.com, November, 2005.

INDEX

A

Accion USA, 58
acquisitions, 200
Adelman, Karen, 175
AdSense, 148, 165-166
advertising. *See* marketing
AdWords, 148
affiliate programs, 163-164
Aigner-Clark, Julie, 102-104
Altpick.com, 174
Amazon.com, 104, 163
AMIBA (American Independent
    Business Alliance), 129
anxieties about risk, setting aside.
    See risk management
Appature, 82
Apple, 16, 186
    iPod, 91, 96
Ashley Stewart, 104
Ashwell, Rachael, 193
Ask the Builder Web site, 165
aspiration gaps, 9-12
aspiration vector, 10
Austin Independent Business
    Alliance, 128
Aveda, 103
Azante Jewelry, 78

B

Baby Einstein, 102-104
Baker, Mary, 151
BALLE (Business Alliance
    for Local Living
    Economics), 129
bank financing, 57-59
Banker to the Poor, 21

benefits, selling, 137
Berlin, Isaiah, 197
Best Buy, 113-116
Beth Bath & Beyond, 116
Bezos, Jeff, 104
Biddulph, Jennifer, 154
big-box retailers, competing against
    big-box retail sales strategies,
        115-116
    differentiation strategies,
        122-123
    independent business
        alliances, 128-129
    Kazoo & Company case
        study, 124-125
    operating in niche
        markets, 120-122
    overview, 113-114, 119-120
    partnering with other small
        businesses, 127-128
    shopping the competition,
        129-131
    stressing locally owned nature
        of business, 125-126
    vulnerabilities of big-box
        stores, 116-119
Black, Kate, 175
blogging, 151-152
Blue Mountain, 167
Bodacious, 102
bootstrap, 51
borrowing money. *See*
    raising money
Boulder Independent Business
    Alliance, 128
Box.net, 170
brainstorming, 106-107
brands, establishing, 141-144

Brin, Sergei, 16
Buffett, Warren, 77
bug report, 107
BurstMedia, 167
Business Alliance for Local Living
    Economics (BALLE), 129
business angels, 60
business experience
  benefits of, 69
  disadvantages of, 71-72
  domain-specific experience, 72-74
  feelings of inadequacy, 70-71
  opportunities with minimal need
    for experience
    businesses with well-established
      business models, 79-81
    direct sales, 77-79
    franchising, 74-76
  overcoming lack of
    online forums, 83-85
    overview, 81
    partnerships, 82-83
    support groups, 83-85
  overview, 67-69
business ideas, finding
  brainstorming, 106-107
  environment trends. *See*
    environmental trends
  gaps in the marketplace, 101-104
  library and Internet research,
    108-109
  myth that the best ideas are
    taken, 87-89
  niche markets, 90
  original versus existing ideas, 105
  overview, 89, 104-105
  unsolved problems, 98-101
business models, 79-81
business opportunities,
    researching, 36-41
business owners. *See also*
    business experience
  characteristics of, 3-6, 25
  loneliness, dealing with, 14-15
  misconception of business owners
    as high-risk takers, 24
  motivation for starting businesses
    aspiration gaps, 9-12
    overview, 6-7
    passion for business
      ideas, 15-20
    self-efficacy, 12-14
    triggering events, 7-9
  support networks, 14-15
business plans, writing, 40-41

C

Cadoo, 188
Candle 79, 18
Candle Café, 18
capabilities of business,
    determining, 185-186
capital constraints, 196-197
Carter, Daren, 75
Carter, Tim, 165
Cartridge World, 8
Carvan, Justin, 95
cash advances, 63
cash flow management, 194-195
Casual Male, 104
Casual Plus, 104
category killer stores, 115
Catster, 90
CD Baby, 196-197
Celiac disease, 18
Chipotle, 104
Christopher, Doris, 46, 77, 182
Ciravolo, Tish, 72-73
Clara Belle Collections, 55
CNN, 10
coaching for new business
    owners, 53-54
Cole, Richard, 101
Collin, Jim, 197
Commission Junction, 164
Common Cause, 88
competing against big-box retailers.
    See big-box retailers,
    competing against
competitions, 62
Complete Idiot's Guide to Running a
    Bed and Breakfast, 80
CompUSA, 184
consumer-driven companies, 143
continuous growth stage (organiza-
    tional life cycle), 193
Contours Express, 75, 103
Cosi, 104
Costco
  sales strategies, 115-116
  vulnerabilities, 117
costs of starting a business. *See*
    startup costs
Count Me In, 58
CraftBuddy.com, 152
Craigslist, 74
Cranium, 139, 188
credibility, building, 140-141
Cruise Planner, 38
Cummings, Josh, 76
Curves, 75, 103
cutting costs, 54-56

D

Daisy Rock Guitars, 72-73, 87
darynkagen.com, 68
Deal of the Day, 167
Dell, Inc., 35, 67
Dell, Michael, 35, 67
Delta Airlines, 8
Design Crowd, 174
diabetes, 33
Dick's Sporting Goods, 117
differentiation strategies, 122-123
direct ads, 166-167
direct sales, 77-79
Direct Selling Association, 78
Discovery Toys, 103
Disney, 102
diverse market methods, 137-140
Dodgers, 14
Dogster, 90
domain-specific experience, 72-74
DoubleClick, 167
Dover Canyon Winery, 151-152
drop-shipping, 168
Druxman, Lisa, 101, 150
Dry Soda, 106
Dwight, Mark, 184
Dynamic Interventions, 11, 68

E

e-commerce, 168-169
early growth stage (organizational
    life cycle), 191-192
eBags, 169
eBay, 81, 201
    affiliate program, 163
    eBay University, 81
EBL Coaching, 32, 52, 192
economic trends, 92-94
Elance, 74, 173
Ellen Tracey, 93
The E-Myth Revisited, 191
endowment effect, 26-28
English, Quentin, 171
entrepreneurs. *See* business owners
environment trends
    economic trends, 92-94
    mattress industry example, 97-98
    overview, 91
    political action and regulatory
        changes, 96-97
    social trends, 94-95
    technological advances, 95-96
equity funding, 60-61
Etsy, 159, 174-175

events that trigger startup of
    businesses, 7-9
excess startup funds, 49-51
experience. *See* business experience
extending product lines, 199
external growth strategies, 200-201
Exterprise, 35

F

Facebook, 94, 153
Fake, Caterina, 45
FedEx, 87
Fields, Kathy, 138
financing new businesses. *See*
    startup costs
finding business ideas. *See*
    business ideas, finding
Firefly Mobile, 99
Flavorx, 17-18, 24-25, 68
Flickr, 45, 170
Flow Corp., 36
forums, online, 83-85
Founders at Work, 47
franchising, 74-76, 200
Free Article Depot, 161
freelance-related Web sites, 172-175
Freelance Switch, 174
Fremont Group, 31
Fremont Ventures, 31

G

Game Neverending, 45
gaps in the marketplace,
    generating business ideas
    from, 101-104
Gardner, John, 88
Gates, Bill, 16, 67
Geeks On Call, 101
geographic expansion, 199
Gerber, Michael E., 191
goals, 30-34
Goff, Mark, 121
Good Housekeeping Seal of
    Approval, 140
Good to Great, 197
Google, 16, 200
    AdSense, 148, 165-166
    AdWords, 148
grants, 61-62
grass roots seeding, 154
Greasecar Vegetable Fuel Systems, 95
GreatCall, Inc., 99-100

growth of businesses
    appreciating nature of, 181-184
    determining business's core
        strengths and capabilities,
        185-186
    overview, 179-181
    planning for, 187-188
    stages of growth. *See*
        organizational life cycle
Gruner, Ron, 47-48
Guaranteed Loan Program, 57
Guru.com, 173

H

H2OAudio, 96
Hahn, Chris, 82
Harris, Arlene, 100
Hazan, Joyce Rita, 36
Headd, Brian, 24
"Hedgehog and the Fox," 197
help for new business owners, 53-54
Hidden Curriculum Education, 61
Home Depot, 113
    sales strategies, 116
    vulnerabilities, 117-119
*How to Open a Financially
    Successful Bed & Breakfast
    or Small Hotel*, 80
*How to Start and Operate Your
    Own Bed-and-Breakfast:
    Down-To-Earth Advice
    from an Award-Winning
    B&B Owner*, 80

I

ideas. *See* business ideas
IHearSafe earbuds, 99
inadequacy, overcoming feelings
    of, 70-71
Inc. magazine, 44
independent business
    alliances, 128-129
Independent Pharmacy
    Cooperative, 127
industry-driven companies, 143
infomercials, 138-139
Ingemi Corp., 99
Ingemi, Christine, 98
Inn Virginia, 80
Intercounty Appliance, 127
internal growth strategies, 198-200

international expansion, 199
Internet advertising, 148-149
Internet bubble, 157
Internet business opportunities
    affiliate programs, 163-164
    direct ads, 166-167
    e-commerce, 168-169
    freelance-related Web
        sites, 172-175
    Internet-related knowledge and
        expertise, acquiring, 159-160
    overview, 157-158, 162-163
    patience, 161-162
    pay-per-click programs, 164-166
    social networking Web sites, 171
    subscription services, 169-170
    users, attracting, 160-161
Internet research, 108-109
introduction stage (organizational
    life cycle), 190-191
iPod, 91, 96

J

J.J. Creations, 118
J.J. Matis, 13
Jingle Network, 100
Jitterbug, 99
Jobs, Steve, 16, 186
Jones, Christopher, 11
Just For Girl's Sports, 117

K

Kagan, Daryn, 10-11, 49
Kalivo, 14
Kawasaki, Guy, 71
Kazoo & Company, 103, 124-125
Kepner-Tregoe, 16
Ketler, Lorna, 102
Khalid, Lubna, 18
Kinzer, Craig, 9
Klause, Sharelle, 106
Kleeman, Jay, 96
Kleeman, Kim, 96
Kleiner Perkins, 60
Kliger, Scott, 100
Kotler, Philip, 88
Kramm, Hadley, 17-18, 24
Kramm, Kenny, 17-18, 24-25
Kroc, Ray, 192

L

LA Gear, 186-187
LaBat, David, 11
lack of experience, overcoming
  online forums, 83-85
  overview, 81
  partnerships, 82-83
  support groups, 83-85
Ladies Who Launch, 14, 54, 192
Lady of America, 103
Larson, Cheri, 78
Lawrence, Bill, 30
learning, vicarious, 13
Lee, Tony, 36
legislation, No Child Left Behind
  Act, 96
Levy, Emily, 31-32, 52, 192
library research, 38, 108-109
licensing, 200
Light, Stephen, 36
LinkShare, 164
Livingston, Jessica, 47
loans. *See* borrowing money
locally owned businesses,
  advertising, 125-126
loneliness, dealing with, 14-15
Long, Dave, 8
Long, Kelly, 9
Los Angeles Dodgers, 14
loss aversion, 26-28
Ludlow, Betsy, 191

M

Madhok, Michelle, 56
magazines, 40
  Inc., 44
  ReadyMade, 37
  SMITH, 37
Magierski, Brian, 14
Make Mine a Million $ Business, 58
marketing
  advertising criteria, 145-146
  blogging, 151-152
  building credibility and
    support, 140-141
  business names, 142-143
  considering diverse marketing
    methods, 137-140
  establishing a brand, 141-144
  Internet advertising, 148-149
  niche markets, 90, 120-122,
    135-136
  overview, 133-135
  print and media advertising,
    146-148
  public relations, 149-151
  selling benefits rather than
    features, 137
  social networking, 152-153
  word-of-mouth marketing, 153-155
Matis, J. J., 13-14
mattress industry, 97-98
Maxwell, Brian, 154-155
May Kay, 35
McAfee ASaP, 139
McDonald's, 76, 137, 192
McGrath, Mary, 11
media advertising, 146-148
Meetup, 84
mergers, 200
Miami Dade Empowerment Trust, 61
microcredit, 21
Microsoft, 16, 67
minimizing startup costs
  overview, 51
  seeking coaching and
    assistance, 53-54
  selecting appropriate business
    to start, 51-53
Mintel, 108
money issues. *See* startup costs
motivating factors for
    starting businesses
  aspiration gaps, 9-12
  overview, 6-7
  passion for business ideas, 15-20
  self-efficacy, 12-14
  triggering events, 7-9
Muchausen, Baron, 51
MyCIO.com, 139
MySpace, 94, 153

N

naming businesses, 142-143
National Association for Women
    Business Owners, 83
nature of growth, appreciating,
    181-184
Nelson, Diana, 124
Nelson, Zach, 139
new product development, 199
NewsCloud, 15
niche markets, 90, 120-122, 135-136
Nichols, Susan, 99
No Child Left Behind Act, 96
Nobel Peace Prize, 21
Nygren, Mike, 14

O

O'Connell, Kristina, 11-12
Oddball Shoe Company, 148, 168
Olivine, 93
1-800-Flowers, 163
100 Percent Napa Valley
    certification mark, 140
onlc.com, 168
online forums, 83-85
OpenTable.com, 95
Oracle Software, 31
Oregon Entrepreneurs Network, 54
organizational life cycle, 189
    capital constraints, 196-197
    cash flow management, 194-195
    continuous growth, 193
    early growth, 191-192
    external growth strategies, 200-201
    internal growth strategies, 198-200
    introduction, 190-191
    price stability, 195
    quality control, 195-196
Origins, 103
overcoming lack of experience
    online forums, 83-85
    overview, 81
    partnerships, 82-83
    support groups, 83-85
Overstock.com, 164

P

p.45 clothing boutique, 102
Page, Larry, 16
Paige's Music, 121
The Pampered Chef, 46, 68,
    77, 87, 182
Panera Bread, 104
part-time businesses, 73
partnerships, 82-83, 127-128
passion for business ideas, 15-20
patience, 161-162
pay-per-click programs, 164-166
PayPal, 201
Peaper, Carleen, 38
Pence, Caprial, 58-59
Pence, John, 58-59
personality- or image-driven
    companies, 143
PetSmart
    sales strategies, 115-116
    vulnerabilities, 117
Philbin, Regis, 27
Pierson, Joy, 18
planning for growth, 187-188

Plaza, John, 16
political action, 96-97
PopCap, 103
Portland Independent Business &
    Community Alliance, 128
PostNet, 76
Powell, Doug, 33-34, 73
Powell, Lisa, 33-34, 73
Powell, Maya, 33-34
PowerBar, 154-155
*Preparing Effective Business
    Plans: An Entrepreneurial
    Approach*, 57
preparing for business growth
    appreciating nature of
        growth, 181-184
    determining business's core
        strengths and capabilities,
        185-186
    planning, 187-188
price stability, 195
print advertising, 146-148
priorities in life, determining, 30-34
Proactiv, 106, 138, 188
product- or service-driven
        companies, 143
Professional Association of
        Innkeepers, 80
Prosper, 58
public relations, 149-151

Q-R

quality control, 195-196
Quentin's Friends, 171

raising money
    bank financing, 57-59
    cash advances, 63
    competitions, 62
    disadvantages of, 48-49
    equity funding, 60-61
    grants, 61-62
    overview, 56-57
ReadyMade, 37
Real Cosmetics, 18, 118
Redfin, 172
Redpoint Ventures, 60
ReferenceUSA, 39
regulatory changes, 96-97
Reifman, Jeff, 15
Rent-A-Wreck, 195
researching business opportunities,
        36-41, 108-109
Rhapsody, 170

risk management
determining what you want out
of life, 30-34
endowment effect, 26-28
having a sense of "what's the worst
thing that can happen," 34-36
loss aversion, 26-28
misconception of business
owners as high-risk takers, 24
nature of risk, 25-28
researching business
opportunities, 36-41
statistics, 23-24
writing business plans, 40-41
Rita Hazan Salon, 36
Roberts, Jan, 120
Rodan, Katie, 106, 138
Rosen, Brian, 123
Rufus Shirts, 190

S

sales
big-box retail sales
strategies, 115-116
direct sales, 77-79
Sally Beauty Supply, 120-122
Sam's Club, 115
Sam's Wine & Spirits, 122
saturation strategy, 116
saving money, 54-56
Saxena, Manoj, 35
SBA Guaranteed Loan Program, 57
SBDC (Small Business Development
Center), 53
SBIR (Small Business Innovation
Research) program, 62
SBIRworld, 62
Scene It?, 8-9
Schultz, Howard, 19
Schwaderer, Sue, 30
Schwartz, Dave, 195
Science, Industry and Business
Library, 39
SCORE (Service Corps of Retired
Executives), 39, 53
Screen Life, 8
Search Engine Optimization
(SEO), 161
SeatGuru, 149
Seattle Biodiesel, 16
Select Comfort, 97
self-efficacy, 12-14
self-esteem, 12

SEO (Search Engine
Optimization), 161
Sephora, 103
Sequoia Capital, 60
Sermo, 172
Service Corps of Retired Executives
(SCORE), 39, 53
7(A) Loan Guaranty Program, 57
Shabby Chic, 193, 199
Shade Clothing, 93
Shahani, Kabir, 82
Shakespeare Squared, 96
ShareASale, 164
Shareholder.com, 47-48
SheFinds, 56
shopping the competition, 129-131
Shutterfly, 170
Silk Soymilk, 141
Simpson, Tom, 19
Singer, April, 190
Sivers, Derek, 197
Slim and Tone, 191
Small Business Administration, 24
Small Business Computing and
E-Commerce Forum, 85
Small Business Development Center
(SBDC), 53
Small Business Innovation Research
(SBIR) program, 62
small business owners. *See* business
owners
Small Business Technology Transfer
(STTR) program, 62
SMITH magazine, 37
Smith, Larry, 37
SmugMug, 170
social networking, 152-153, 171
social trends, 94-95
Sohl, Jeffrey, 60
Sologig.com, 173
Sonneborn, Marcene, 107
South West Trading Co., 95
Southwest Airlines, 142
So—You Want to Be an Innkeeper, 80
Spangler, Steve, 152
SPC Office Products, 103
stages of growth. *See*
organizational life cycle
Starbucks, 19, 142
startup costs
average startup cost, 43
limited startup funds, 45-48
minimizing
*cutting costs and saving
money, 54-56*
overview, 51

seeking coaching and
assistance, 53-54
selecting appropriate business
to start, 51-53
overview, 43-44
raising/borrowing money. *See*
raising money
StartupNation, 84
StartupJournal, 36
Steve Spangler Science, 152
Steve Spangler's Secrets (blog), 152
Stone, Kenneth, 118, 122
strategic alliances, 200
strengths of business,
determining, 185-186
stressing locally owned nature of
business, 125-126
Stroller Strides, 101, 150
STTR (Small Business Technology
Transfer) program, 62
subscription services, 169-170
Sullivan, Hannah, 31
support, building, 140-141
support groups, 83-85
support networks, 14-15

T

Tahoe Trips & Trails, 31
Target, 115-116
technological advances, 95-96
TechStudents.com, 168
Tempur-Pedic International, 97
Tennant, Sean, 8
Timbuk2, 184
Tory Burch, 93
Tranquil Space, 32
trends, environmental. *See*
environmental trends
Tribal Fusion, 167
triggering events, 7-9
Trivial Pursuit, 139
Troget, Benjamin, 16
Tupperware, 35
Type 1 and Type 2 Tools, 34, 73
type 1 diabetes, 33
TypePad Pro, 151

U

U.S. Cycling Team, 155
U.S. Small Business
Administration, 24
Udall, Laura, 99, 104, 136-137

UFOC (Uniform Franchise Offering
Circular), 76
UL (Underwriters Laboratories), 140
unsolved problems, generating
business ideas from, 98-101
users, attracting to Internet
businesses, 160-161

V

value loop retailing, 115-116
venture capitalists, 60
Venture Lab, 54
vicarious learning, 13
Vieira, Meredith, 27
Visa Business Breakthrough
Contest, 62
vulnerabilities of big-box
stores, 116-119

W

Wadee, 11-12, 118, 168
Wal-Mart, 68, 113-119
Walton, Sam, 129
WebShots, 170
Weddle's, 148
Westmoreland Bistro, 59
Wheelworks, 123
White Wave, 141
"Who Wants to Be a
Millionaire?," 27-28
Wilkins, Barb, 102
Williams, Clara Rankin, 55
Williams, Rozalia, 61
Wilson, Kimberly, 32
Wisconsin Bed and Breakfast
Association, 80
word-of-mouth marketing, 153-155
writing business plans, 40-41

X-Y-Z

Yahoo!, 46, 157
Yogitoes, 99
Yunus, Muhammad, 21

Zazzle.com, 175
Zook, Chris, 179
ZUCA, 99, 104, 136-137